A Taste of the Great Outdoors

Cooking on the Go
for RVs, Motor Coaches, Camping & Picnics

Jacquie Schmit   Eileen Mandryk   Jo Wuth

Three Sisters Publishing Inc.

A Taste of the Great Outdoors

by

Jacquie Schmit 🌲 Eileen Mandryk 🌲 Jo Wuth

Second Printing – January 2003

Copyright © 2000 by
Three Sisters Publishing Inc.
12234 – 49 Street
Edmonton, Alberta
Canada T5W 3A8
www.3sistersbooks.com

CANADIAN CATALOGUING IN PUBLICATION DATA
Schmit, Jacquie

A taste of the great outdoors

Includes index.
ISBN 1-894022-58-0

1. Quick and easy cookery.   2. Outdoor cookery.
3. Recreational vehicle living.   4. Camping.
I. Mandryk, Eileen   II. Wuth, Jo   III. Title.

TX823.S36 2000   641.5'75   C00-920225-0

Photography by:
Merle Prosofsky, Merle Prosofsky Photography, Edmonton, Alberta

Dishes, Accessories and Flowers courtesy of:
Call the Kettle Black, Edmonton, Alberta
Camper's Village, Edmonton, Alberta
Greenland Garden Centre, Sherwood Park, Alberta

Page Formatting and Index by Iona Glabus

Designed, Printed and Produced in Canada by:
Centax Books, a Division of PrintWest Communications Ltd.
Publishing Director, Photo Designer & Food Stylist: Margo Embury
1150 Eighth Avenue, Regina, Saskatchewan, Canada S4R 1C9
(306) 525-2304   FAX (306) 757-2439
E-mail: centax@printwest.com   www.centaxbooks.com

Table of Contents

Recipes have been tested in U.S. Standard measurements. Common metric measurements are given as a convenience for those who are more familiar with metric. Recipes have not been tested in metric.

Introduction

Because it is my turn, and because I seriously lack the talent the other two sisters possess for writing poems and verses, I can only write what is in my heart. We wish to dedicate this cookbook, our third, to our Mother for it was she who instilled in all of us, each in our own way, our profound love of cooking, nature and the great outdoors.

A British, pioneer-spirited lady, Mom nurtured with pride her flower and vegetable gardens; canning, freezing and preserving every imaginable fruit and vegetable that northern Alberta soil would produce. Her favorite time of year was when she watched in awe as her little seedlings turned into the imaginative dishes she loved to cook for her family.

The death of our father left Mom a young widow. She took her many culinary skills and went on to cook professionally at Camp He Ho Ha on Lake Isle. Again combining her passions for cooking and nature.

At the age of 92, Mom passed away in June 2000. She would have loved this cookbook for it combines our love of nature with our love of good food.

Mom, this one is for you!

by Jacquie Schmit for the Sisters Three

We were born and raised the Campbell girls in the farming community of Lamont, Alberta. Our first book *A Taste of Christmas* reflects the special magical times of our family Christmas traditions. Our second book *A Taste of Brunch* is a tempting, no-fuss collection of our favorite brunch recipes to share with your family and friends all year long. We hope that you will enjoy this new collection of our recipes for people on the move as you escape from the everyday in your RV, motor coach, camper, or just for a relaxed picnic or backyard feast.

Make-Ahead Treats
(Preparing to Move Out)

Mixes

Biscuits & Muffins

Cookies & Bars

Cakes

Honey Cinnamon Popcorn Mix

A sweet and spicy treat, children love this snack mix.

6 cups	popped popcorn	1.5 L
2 cups	chow mein noodles	500 mL
5 tbsp.	butter OR margarine	75 mL
3 tbsp.	sugar	45 mL
1 tsp.	vanilla	5 mL
½ tsp.	ground cinnamon	2 mL
2 cups	roasted whole almonds	500 mL
1 cup	raisins, washed and dried	250 mL

Preheat oven to 250°F (120°C). In a large shallow roasting pan, combine popcorn and chow mein noodles. In a small saucepan, over low heat, melt butter and sugar. Stir in vanilla and cinnamon; mix well. Remove from heat and pour over popcorn mixture, toss to coat. Bake 1 hour, stirring gently every 15 minutes. Stir in almonds and raisins. Remove from oven and cool completely. Store in an airtight container.

Makes 10 cups (2.5 L)

Cajun Nut and Cereal Snack Mix

Jacquie likes it hot. These spicy nibbles you can enjoy all year round.

2½ cups	bite-sized corn cereal squares	625 mL
2 cups	bite-sized rice cereal squares	500 mL
2 cups	Crispix cereal	500 mL
1 cup	mini pretzels	250 mL
1 cup	mixed nuts	250 mL
1 cup	whole cashews	250 mL
½ cup	butter OR margarine, melted	125 mL
1 tbsp.	dried parsley flakes	15 mL
1 tsp.	celery salt	5 mL
2 tsp.	garlic powder	10 mL
¼ tsp.	cayenne pepper	1 mL
½ tsp.	hot pepper sauce	2 mL

Cajun Nut and Cereal Snack Mix Continued

Preheat oven to 250°F (120°C). In a large bowl, combine all cereals, pretzels and nuts; toss to combine well. In a small bowl, combine melted butter, parsley flakes, celery salt, garlic powder, cayenne pepper and hot pepper sauce; stir well and pour over the cereal mixture. Stir gently to coat. Pour the cereal nut mix into a 10 x 15" (25 x 38 cm) ungreased baking pan. Bake for 40-60 minutes, stirring every 15 minutes. Allow to cool completely. Store in airtight containers.

Makes 9 cups (2.25 L)

Deviled Trail Mix

This is great for when the munchies hit while travelling.

3 cups	bite-sized wheat cereal squares	750 mL
3 cups	bite-sized corn cereal squares	750 mL
3	plain rice cakes, in bite-sized pieces	3
2 cups	pretzel sticks	500 mL
3 tbsp.	vegetable oil	45 mL
1 tbsp.	Worcestershire sauce	15 mL
2 tsp.	chili powder	10 mL
2 tsp.	dry mustard	10 mL
1 tsp.	garlic powder	5 mL

Preheat oven to 350°F (180°C). In a large bowl, combine cereals, rice cakes and pretzel sticks; stir to combine and set aside. In a small bowl, combine oil, Worcestershire sauce, chili powder, mustard and garlic powder. Stir well and pour over the cereal mixture. Toss to coat. Pour into a 10 x 15" (25 x 38 cm) baking dish. Bake for 20-25 minutes, or until Trail Mix is crisp and golden. Stir several times during baking period.

Cool completely. Store Trail Mix in a tightly covered container.

Makes 10 cups (2.5 mL)

Golden Granola

This is incredibly versatile. It may be eaten as a cereal; used to top ice cream, puddings or fruit, or eat as is while hiking or back packing.

4 cups	rolled oats	1 L
1 cup	flaked coconut	250 mL
½ cup	wheat germ	125 mL
½ cup	sesame seeds	125 mL
½ cup	sunflower seeds	125 mL
½ cup	slivered almonds OR Brazil nuts	125 mL
1½ tsp.	salt	7 mL
1½ tsp.	ground cinnamon	7 mL
½ cup	vegetable oil	125 mL
¼ cup	brown sugar	60 mL
⅓ cup	liquid honey	75 mL
⅓ cup	water	75 mL
1 tbsp.	vanilla	15 mL
½ cup	raisins, washed and dried	125 mL
½ cup	chopped dried apricots OR dried fruit of choice	125 mL

Preheat oven to 275°F (140°C). In a large bowl, combine oats, coconut, wheat germ, sesame seeds, sunflower seeds, almonds, salt and cinnamon; mix well. In a small saucepan, combine oil, brown sugar, honey, water and vanilla; set over medium-low heat and cook, stirring constantly, until sugar is dissolved and mixture is smooth. Pour over the dry ingredients and mix well. Pour granola mixture into a lightly buttered 9 x 13" (23 x 33 cm) baking pan. Bake for 1 hour, or until golden, stirring every 15 minutes. Cool completely. Stir in raisins and apricots. Store the granola in a tightly covered container. Refrigerated it will keep up to 2 weeks.

Makes 9 cups (2.25 L)

Pictured on page 17.

Basic Baking Mix

9 cups	flour	2.25 L
⅓ cup	baking powder	75 mL
4 tsp.	salt	20 mL
2 cups	butter OR margarine	500 mL

In a large bowl, combine flour, baking powder and salt. Cut in butter with a pastry blender or 2 knives until the mixture resembles fine crumbs. Store in a covered container in the refrigerator. Use as follows:

Makes about 10 cups (2.5 L)

To Make Biscuits and Shortcakes: Preheat oven to 400°F (200°C). Combine 2 cups (500 mL) of baking mix with ½ cup (125 mL) milk. Stir only until the dough clings together. Pat out or roll dough to ½" (1.3 cm) thickness. Cut with 2½" (6 cm) cutter into 12 rounds. Place rounds on an ungreased baking sheet. Bake for 10-12 minutes

Variations: For **Drop Biscuits:** Prepare as above, increasing milk to ¾ cup (175 mL). Add chopped fresh or dried herbs and grated cheese if you wish. Drop heaping tablespoons (20 mL) of dough onto an ungreased baking sheet. Bake as above.

To Make Pancakes: Combine 2 cups (500 mL) of baking mix with 1¾ cups (425 mL) milk and 2 eggs. Stir just until moistened. Spoon batter onto griddle and spread cakes to the size you want. Turn when bubbles break, approximately 2-3 minutes. Cook for an additional 1-2 minutes. Serve immediately. Makes 12 pancakes

Variation: For **Fruit Pancakes**: Add to batter just before cooking, ½-¾ cup (125-175 mL) drained blueberries, strawberries, or raspberries, or ½-¾ cup (125-175 mL) finely diced apple.

Variation: For feather-light pancakes, substitute club soda for the milk.

To Make Dumplings: Combine 1 cup (250 mL) of baking mix with ½ cup (125 mL) milk. Stir just until moistened. Drop by large spoonfuls into simmering liquid; cover and cook for 20 minutes. Do not peek until done. Makes 6 dumplings

Variation: For **Herbed Dumplings**, add 1 tsp. (5 mL) dried or 1 tbsp. (15 mL) fresh chopped herbs, dillweed, parsley, thyme, etc. to dumpling batter.

Bacon and Cheddar Biscuits

These biscuits are always in demand. They can be frozen and reheated in a microwave, toaster oven, grill or over a campfire. Make two batches and freeze one.

5 slices	bacon, cooked crisp and crumbled	5 slices
2¼ cups	flour	500 mL
4 tsp.	baking powder	20 mL
½ tsp.	salt	2 mL
½ cup	butter OR margarine	125 mL
½ cup	grated Cheddar cheese	125 mL
1 cup	milk	250 mL

Glaze:

1	egg yolk, lightly beaten	1
¼ cup	grated Cheddar cheese	60 mL

Cook the bacon. Preheat oven to 450°F (230°C). In a large bowl, combine flour, baking powder and salt. Using a pastry blender or 2 knives, cut in butter until mixture is crumbly. Add cheese and bacon; toss lightly to combine. Gradually add milk, stirring with a fork to make a soft dough. Add more milk if necessary to moisten all dry ingredients. Turn out dough onto a floured work surface and knead for 8-10 turns. Pat out dough to ½" (1.3 cm) thickness; cut into 2½" (6 cm) rounds with a biscuit or cookie cutter. Place on an ungreased cookie sheet. Brush biscuits with egg yolk and sprinkle with cheese. Bake for 10-15 minutes, or until golden brown. Serve warm with butter.

Makes 12 biscuits

Pictured on page 85.

🌲 **Eat your most perishable items, fresh foods and meats, first so they don't spoil.**

Cheddar Dill Muffins

A savory cheese muffin with a hint of dill. Wonderful with soups or salads; ideal as a breakfast muffin.

2 cups	flour	500 mL
½ cup	sugar	125 mL
1 tbsp.	baking powder	15 mL
1 tsp.	salt	5 mL
½ tsp.	baking soda	2 mL
1 tsp.	dillweed	5 mL
1¼ cups	shredded sharp Cheddar cheese	425 mL
2	eggs	2
1 cup	plain yogurt OR sour cream	250 mL
¼ cup	butter OR margarine, melted	60 mL

Preheat oven to 400°F (200°C). In a large bowl, combine flour, sugar, baking powder, salt, baking soda and dillweed; stir well. Add cheese and toss to combine. In a separate bowl, with an electric mixer, beat eggs until frothy. Add yogurt and melted butter; mix well. Add to dry ingredients all at once and stir just until moistened. Spoon batter into lightly buttered large muffin cups, filling ¾ full. Bake for 20-25 minutes, or until a cake tester inserted in center of muffin comes out clean. Remove from oven and allow muffins to sit in pan for 10-15 minutes. Transfer muffins to a wire rack to cool completely. Serve warm or cold.

Makes 12 large muffins

Variation: Omit the dillweed; increase cheese to 2 cups (500 mL) and add a 1 oz. (28 g) package of Ranch Dressing Mix to the dry ingredients. Mix and bake as above.

Pictured on page 35.

Hot Corn Muffins

A zesty breakfast treat to wake up your tastebuds.

1 cup	flour	250 mL
1 cup	cornmeal	250 mL
2 tbsp.	sugar	30 mL
2½ tsp.	baking powder	12 mL
½ tsp.	salt	2 mL
1 cup	milk	250 mL
½ cup	vegetable oil	125 mL
2	eggs, lightly beaten	2
1 tsp.	hot pepper sauce	5 mL
1 cup	corn kernels, canned, drained; OR thawed, frozen	250 mL

Preheat oven to 400°F (200°C). In a large bowl, combine flour, cornmeal, sugar, baking powder and salt; mix well. In a separate bowl, combine milk, oil, eggs and hot pepper sauce; stir well. Make a well in center of dry ingredients; add the milk mixture and stir just to combine. Stir in corn. Spoon batter into 12 lightly buttered large muffin cups. Bake for 15-25 minutes, or until a cake tester inserted in center comes out clean. Remove from oven and cool for 5 minutes in pans. Remove from pans to a wire rack. Serve warm.

Makes 12 large muffins

Organize yourself to do as many make-ahead items as possible. Cookies, muffins, biscuits, breads, many salads and main dishes can be made at home and easily packed.

Orange Bran Muffins

Wholesome, nutritious muffins with a hint of orange, these are guaranteed to wake up your morning tastebuds.

2 cups	natural bran	500 mL
1 cup	flour	250 mL
¼ cup	wheat germ	60 mL
2 tsp.	baking soda	10 mL
½ tsp.	salt	2 mL
1 cup	chopped dates	250 mL
½ cup	chopped pecans	125 mL
1 tbsp.	grated orange rind	15 mL
⅓ cup	vegetable oil	75 mL
⅓ cup	molasses OR corn syrup	75 mL
1¾ cups	buttermilk	425 mL

Preheat oven to 400°F (200°C). In a large bowl, combine bran, flour, wheat germ, baking soda and salt. Add dates, pecans and orange rind; toss lightly to combine and to coat dates. In a small bowl, combine oil, molasses and buttermilk; stir to combine and pour over dry ingredients. Stir just until moistened. Pour into 12 lightly buttered, or paper-lined large muffin cups, filling each cup to the top. Bake for 25-30 minutes, or until firm to the touch. Remove muffins from oven and transfer to a wire rack to cool. Store in a covered container for 1-2 days, or wrap well and freeze.

Makes 12 large muffins

Measure and combine dry ingredients, including spices, for all meals ahead of time. Place them in resealable sandwich bags. Be sure to label the bags!

Blueberry and Banana Muffins

Use wild blueberries when you can find them, the flavor is much more intense and they are especially wonderful in this recipe.

1 cup	mashed ripe bananas (2 medium bananas)	250 mL
2	eggs	2
1 cup	brown sugar	250 mL
½ cup	butter OR margarine, melted	125 mL
1 cup	blueberries	250 mL
1 tsp.	vanilla	5 mL
2¼ cups	flour	550 mL
2 tsp.	baking powder	10 mL
½ tsp.	ground cinnamon	2 mL
½ tsp.	salt	2 mL

Preheat oven to 350°F (180°C). In a large bowl, combine mashed bananas, eggs, sugar and melted butter; mix well. Stir in blueberries and vanilla. In a separate bowl, combine flour, baking powder, cinnamon and salt; stir well. Stir banana mixture into flour mixture until evenly moistened. Spoon batter into 12 lightly buttered large muffin tins. Bake for 25-30 minutes, or until a cake tester when inserted in the center comes out clean. Serve warm.

Makes 12 large muffins

🌲 Always pack matches in a waterproof container.

Peachy Pecan Muffins

Moist and flavorful with a crunchy, nutty topping. You can also make these with canned peaches when fresh are unavailable, but do try them in peach season.

Pecan Cinnamon Topping:

½ cup	chopped pecans	125 mL
⅓ cup	brown sugar	75 mL
¼ cup	flour	60 mL
1 tsp.	ground cinnamon	5 mL
2 tbsp.	butter OR margarine, melted	30 mL

Muffins:

1½ cups	flour	375 mL
½ cup	sugar	125 mL
2 tsp.	baking powder	10 mL
1 tsp.	ground cinnamon	5 mL
½ tsp.	salt	2 mL
½ cup	butter OR margarine, melted	125 mL
¼ cup	milk	60 mL
1	egg	1
1 cup	fresh peaches, peeled, diced (2 medium peaches)	250 mL

Preheat oven to 400°F (200°C).

Topping: In a small bowl, combine chopped pecans, brown sugar, flour and cinnamon; stir well. Add melted butter; stir until mixture is crumbly. Set aside.

Muffin Batter: In a large bowl, combine flour, sugar, baking powder, cinnamon and salt; stir well. In a separate bowl, combine butter, milk and egg; stir well. Pour milk mixture into flour mixture and stir just until moistened. Fold in peaches. Spoon batter into 12 lightly buttered large muffin cups. Sprinkle topping over batter. Bake for 20-30 minutes, or until a cake tester inserted in the center comes out clean. Remove muffins from the pan to a wire rack to cool completely. Store muffins in an airtight container or wrap well and freeze.

Makes 12 large muffins

Banana Macadamia Nut Bread

There is a delicious taste of the tropics in this easy-to-make loaf. It keeps and packs well.

2 cups	flour	500 mL
¾ cup	sugar	175 mL
½ cup	butter OR margarine, softened	125 mL
2	eggs	2
1 tsp.	baking soda	5 mL
½ tsp.	salt	2 mL
1 tbsp.	grated orange rind	15 mL
1 tsp.	vanilla	5 mL
1 cup	mashed ripe bananas (2 medium bananas)	250 mL
¼ cup	orange juice	60 mL
1 cup	flaked coconut	250 mL
¾ cup	coarsely chopped macadamia nuts OR pecans	175 mL

Preheat oven to 350°F (180°C). In a large bowl, combine flour, sugar, butter, eggs, baking soda, salt, orange rind and vanilla. With an electric mixer, beat at low speed, scraping bowl often until well mixed, 2-3 minutes. Add bananas and orange juice. Continuing beating until well mixed, 1-2 minutes. Stir in coconut and nuts. (Batter will be thick.)

Spread batter in a lightly buttered 5 x 9" (13 x 23 cm) loaf pan. Bake for 60-65 minutes, or until cake tester inserted in center comes out clean. Remove from oven; cool in pan for 10 minutes. Remove loaf from pan to a wire rack to cool completely. Wrap well and refrigerate for 3-4 days or freeze for up to 1 month.

Makes 1 loaf

Campfire Breakfast

Campfire Scrambled Eggs, page 40
Bannock on a Stick, page 120
Golden Granola, page 8

Date and Nut Loaf with Orange Glaze

A super moist and delicious loaf for breakfast, brunch or just coffee on the patio.
This loaf keeps and packs well.

1 cup	butter OR margarine, softened	250 mL
2 cups	sugar	500 mL
3	eggs, lightly beaten	3
1 tsp.	vanilla	5 mL
4 cups	flour	1 L
1 tsp.	baking soda	5 mL
1 tsp.	salt	5 mL
1⅓ cups	buttermilk	325 mL
1 cup	chopped walnuts OR pecans	250 mL
1 cup	chopped dates	250 mL
1 tbsp.	grated orange rind	15 mL

Orange Glaze:

¼ cup	orange juice	60 mL
½ cup	sugar	125 mL
2 tbsp.	grated orange rind	30 mL

Preheat oven to 350°F (180°C). In a large bowl, cream butter and sugar; add eggs and vanilla; beat well. Combine flour, baking soda and salt; add to creamed mixture alternately with buttermilk. Fold in walnuts, dates and orange rind. Pour batter into 2 lightly buttered and floured 4½ x 8½" (12 x 22 cm) loaf pans. Bake for 60-65 minutes, or until a cake tester inserted in the center comes out clean.

Glaze: In a small bowl, combine orange juice, sugar and rind. Spoon half the glaze over the hot baked bread. Cool the bread in the pans for 10 minutes; remove from pans and spoon remaining glaze over bread. Loaves may be wrapped well and frozen for up to 2 months.

Makes 2 loaves

Oatmeal Butterscotch Crisps

A crunchy, oat, butterscotch cookie with a hint of cinnamon, it packs well for any outdoor activity.

1¼ cups	flour	300 mL
1 tsp.	baking soda	5 mL
½ tsp.	salt	2 mL
1 tsp.	ground cinnamon	5 mL
1 cup	butter OR margarine, softened	250 mL
¾ cup	sugar	175 mL
¾ cup	brown sugar	175 mL
2	eggs	2
1 tsp.	vanilla	5 mL
3 cups	rolled oats	750 mL
2 cups	butterscotch chips	500 mL

Preheat oven to 375°F (190°C). In a small bowl, combine flour, baking soda, salt and cinnamon; set aside. In a large bowl, with an electric mixer, beat butter and sugars until light and fluffy. Add eggs and vanilla and beat well. Gradually beat in flour mixture; combine well. Stir in oats and butterscotch chips. Drop dough by rounded tablespoonfuls (20 mL) onto ungreased cookie sheets. Bake on the middle rack for 8-10 minutes. Remove cookies from cookie sheets onto wire racks to cool. When cool, cookies may be stored in freezer containers and frozen for up to 2 months.

Makes 48 cookies

When you are camping, plan for simple, filling meals with easy preparation and minimal clean up. Create menus for all of the meals during your camping trip.

Peanut Crisps

This crunchy cookie has loads of peanuts. It keeps well and travels well, great for coffee breaks along the trail.

1 cup	sugar	250 mL
1 cup	brown sugar, firmly packed	250 mL
¾ cup	butter OR margarine, softened	175 mL
1 tsp.	vanilla	5 mL
2	eggs	2
2¼ cups	flour	550 mL
2 cups	rolled oats	500 mL
1 tsp.	baking powder	5 mL
1 tsp.	baking soda	5 mL
1 cup	chopped salted peanuts	250 mL

In a large bowl, combine sugars and butter. With an electric mixer, beat at medium speed until light and fluffy. Add vanilla; add eggs, one at a time, beating well after each addition. Add flour, rolled oats, baking powder and baking soda. Beat at low speed until a soft dough forms. Stir in peanuts. Cover dough with plastic wrap and chill in refrigerator for 1-2 hours.

Preheat oven to 375°F (190°C). Shape dough into 1" (2.5 cm) balls and place on ungreased cookie sheets. Bake on the middle rack for 12-15 minutes, or until golden brown. Cool cookies completely before storing. May be well wrapped and frozen for up to 2 months.

Makes 60 cookies

Variation: For **Chocolate Chip Crisps**, omit the peanuts and add 1½ cups (375 mL) of chocolate chips to the batter.

Pictured on page 103.

Crunchy Cornflake Cookies

This crisp crunchy cookie is a hit with everyone and packs well for outings.

1½ cups	flour	375 mL
½ cup	sugar	125 mL
¼ cup	firmly packed brown sugar	60 mL
½ tsp.	baking soda	2 mL
½ tsp.	salt	2 mL
⅔ cup	butter OR margarine, softened	150 mL
1 tsp.	vanilla	5 mL
2	eggs, lightly beaten	2
1½ cups	cornflakes cereal, crushed to 1 cup (250 mL)	375 mL
½ cup	medium-flake coconut	125 mL
½ cup	chopped walnuts OR pecans	125 mL

Preheat oven to 350°F (180°C). In a large bowl, combine flour, sugar, brown sugar, baking soda and salt; stir well. Add butter. With an electric mixer, beat at medium speed until crumbly. Add vanilla and egg; mix well. Stir in cornflakes, coconut and nuts. Shape dough into 1" (2.5 cm) balls and place on lightly buttered cookie sheets. Flatten slightly with a fork or the bottom of a glass. Bake on the middle rack for 10-15 minutes, or until light golden brown. Remove cookies from oven and let cool for 1-2 minutes in pan. Remove from cookie sheets to cool completely. May be wrapped and frozen for up to 2 months.

Makes 36 cookies

Variation: Substitute a combination of your favorite cereal flakes for the cornflakes.

Health Cookies

This moist nutritious cookie is great for taking with you hiking or back packing.

4	ripe, medium bananas	4
⅓ cup	vegetable oil	75 mL
1 tsp.	vanilla	5 mL
1	orange, grated rind of	1
1½ cups	quick rolled oats	375 mL
1½ cups	chopped mixed dried fruit: raisins, apricots, dates, figs	375 mL
¾ cup	whole-wheat flour	175 mL
½ cup	chopped almonds	125 mL

Preheat oven to 350°F (180°C). In a large mixing bowl, mash the bananas; add oil, vanilla and orange rind. Mix well. Combine oats, dried fruit, flour and almonds; stir into banana mixture. Mix well. Drop dough by teaspoonfuls (5 mL) onto lightly buttered baking sheets. Flatten slightly with a fork. Bake on the middle rack for 20-25 minutes, or until lightly browned. Immediately remove cookies from pan to a wire rack to cool completely. Store in an airtight container in the refrigerator or wrap well and freeze for up to 2 months.

Makes 48 cookies

Pictured on page 103.

Combine recipe ingredients for appropriate recipes at home in resealable plastic bags. Get everything together but the water. Write cooking instructions on the bag or insert a recipe card into the bag, if you need one. This saves time and cuts down on packaging and extra weight to carry. The plastic bags can also be reused.

Spiced Pumpkin Cookies with Penuche Frosting

This nice moist cookie keeps well and travels well. Penuche (pu-noo-chee), a creamy brown sugar frosting or candy, is a delicious bonus.

1 cup	butter OR margarine, softened	250 mL
½ cup	firmly packed brown sugar	125 mL
½ cup	sugar	125 mL
1	egg, lightly beaten	1
1 cup	canned pumpkin	250 mL
1 tsp.	vanilla	5 mL
2 cups	flour	500 mL
1 tsp.	EACH baking soda and baking powder	5 mL
¼ tsp.	salt	1 mL
1 tsp.	ground cinnamon	5 mL
¼ tsp.	EACH ground cloves and nutmeg	1 mL
1 cup	chopped pecans or walnuts	250 mL

Penuche Frosting:

3 tbsp.	butter OR margarine	45 mL
½ cup	firmly packed brown sugar	125 mL
¼ cup	milk	60 mL
1½-2 cups	icing (confectioner's) sugar	375-500 mL

Preheat oven to 350°F (180°C). In a large bowl, with an electric mixer, cream together butter and sugars. Beat until light and fluffy. Add egg and beat well. Add pumpkin and vanilla and beat until well combined. Add flour, baking soda, baking powder, salt, cinnamon, cloves and nutmeg; mix well. Stir in nuts. Drop the dough by rounded teaspoonfuls (7 mL) onto ungreased cookie sheets. Bake on the middle rack for 10-12 minutes, or until light golden brown. Immediately remove the cookies from the cookie sheets to cool.

Frosting: In a small saucepan, combine butter and brown sugar; place over medium heat and bring to a boil. Cook and stir for 1 minute, or until slightly thickened. Cool for 10 minutes; add milk and beat until smooth. Beat in icing sugar until of spreading consistency. Frost cooled cookies. Allow frosting to set before storing cookies.

Makes 60 cookies

Orange Oat Chewies

This chewy cookie has nuts, coconut and a hint of orange. They pack and keep well.

2 cups	brown sugar	500 mL
1 cup	butter OR margarine	250 mL
1 tbsp.	grated orange rind	15 mL
3 tbsp.	frozen orange juice concentrate, thawed	45 mL
2	eggs	2
2 cups	flour	500 mL
1 tsp.	baking soda	5 mL
1 tsp.	salt	5 mL
2 cups	rolled oats	500 mL
1 cup	chopped pecans OR walnuts	250 mL
½ cup	flaked coconut	125 mL

Preheat oven to 350°F (180°C). In a large bowl, with an electric mixer, cream together sugar and butter. Add orange rind, orange juice concentrate and eggs; beat until well mixed and light and fluffy. Combine flour, baking soda and salt; mix well. Add to sugar mixture; beat until well blended. Stir in rolled oats, chopped nuts and coconut; mix well. Drop dough by rounded teaspoonfuls (7 mL) 2" (5 cm) apart on lightly buttered cookie sheets. Bake on the middle rack for 10-12 minutes, or until light golden brown. Cool cookies for 1 minute on cookie sheets; remove to wire racks to cool completely. Store in a tightly covered container or wrap well and freeze for up to 2 months.

Makes 60 cookies

When buying bags of ice cubes for your cooler, keep cubes in the bags rather than spreading them in the cooler, they will stay frozen longer and keep your food cold longer.

Double Chocolate Cookies

A chocolate lover's delight, make a batch for your next camping trip. They pack and keep well.

2 cups	semisweet chocolate chips	500 mL
2 x 1 oz.	squares unsweetened chocolate	2 x 30 g
2 tbsp.	butter	30 mL
2	eggs	2
⅔ cup	sugar	150 mL
1 tsp.	vanilla	5 mL
¼ cup	flour	60 mL
¼ tsp.	baking powder	1 mL
¼ tsp.	salt	1 mL
1 cup	chopped pecans	250 mL

Preheat oven to 350°F (180°C). In a saucepan over low heat, melt 1 cup (250 mL) of chocolate chips, unsweetened chocolate and butter, stirring constantly. Cool slightly. Add eggs, sugar and vanilla; with an electric mixer, beat well. Combine flour, baking powder and salt; add to chocolate mixture and beat well. Stir in remaining chocolate chips and nuts. Drop dough by heaping teaspoonfuls (7 mL) onto lightly buttered cookie sheets. Bake on the middle rack for 8-10 minutes, or until edges are firm and surface is dull and cracked. Remove cookies from the oven and allow to cool on cookie sheets for 1-2 minutes. Transfer to wire racks and cool completely. Store in an airtight container or wrap well and freeze for up to 2 months.

Makes 36 cookies

When camping or backpacking, store food carefully and wipe up spills. Never sleep with food or other items in your tent that may attract bears or other animals (like toothpaste, gum, etc.) – hang them in a bag from a high tree limb.

White Chocolate Chunk Cookies

White chocolate and macadamia nuts - a classic combination for a sophisticated treat.

½ cup	butter OR margarine, softened	125 mL
½ cup	brown sugar	125 mL
¼ cup	sugar	60 mL
1	egg	1
1 tsp.	vanilla	5 mL
1¼ cups	flour	300 mL
½ tsp.	baking soda	2 mL
½ tsp.	salt	2 mL
1 cup	coarsely chopped white chocolate	250 mL
1 cup	coarsely chopped macadamia nuts	250 mL

Preheat oven to 375°F (190°C). In a large bowl, with an electric mixer, beat butter with sugars until light and fluffy. Add egg and vanilla and beat until well combined. Add flour, baking soda and salt; mix well. Stir in chocolate chunks and nuts; mix well. Drop dough by heaping teaspoonfuls (7 mL) onto ungreased cookie sheets. With a fork or pancake turner, flatten each cookie to make a 2" (5 cm) round. Bake on the middle rack for 10-15 minutes, or until lightly browned. Transfer cookies to a wire rack to cool. Cookies may be stored in a tightly covered container or may be wrapped well and frozen for up to 2 months.

Makes 30 cookies

Make an inexpensive welcome mat for your RV or tent from a piece of artificial turf. It will help keep your "outdoor" home clean by picking up loose soil, leaves, etc.

Chocolate Chewy Granola Treats

½ cup	butter OR margarine, softened	125 mL
1 cup	brown sugar	250 mL
1	egg	1
1½ tsp.	vanilla	7 mL
1 cup	flour	250 mL
½ tsp.	baking soda	2 mL
¼ tsp.	salt	1 mL
1 tsp.	ground cinnamon	5 mL
¼ cup	milk	60 mL
2 cups	granola	500 mL
1½ cups	chocolate chips or mini baking bits	375 mL

Preheat oven to 350°F (180°C). In a large bowl, with an electric mixer, cream butter and sugar until light. Add egg and vanilla and beat until light and fluffy. Combine flour, baking soda, salt and cinnamon; stir into creamed mixture alternately with milk. Mix well. Stir in granola and chocolate chips; mix well. Spread the granola mixture in a lightly buttered 10 x 15" (25 x 38 cm) baking pan. Bake on the middle rack for 25-35 minutes, or until golden brown. Remove from oven and cool completely. Cut into bars. Store in a tightly covered container.

Makes 48 bars

Pictured on page 103.

Chewy Honey Granola Bars

As long as you have the granola, this recipe is simple enough to make over a campfire.

5 cups	Golden Granola, page 8	1.25 L
½ cup	whole-wheat flour	125 mL
½ cup	brown sugar	125 mL
½ cup	butter OR margarine	125 mL
⅓ cup	honey	75 mL

Chewy Honey Granola Bars Continued

In a large bowl, combine granola and flour; stir well and set aside. In a small saucepan, combine brown sugar, butter and honey. Set over medium heat and bring to a boil, stirring constantly. Pour sugar syrup over the granola mixture, Stir until granola is well coated. Press into a lightly buttered 9 x 13" (23 x 33 cm) baking pan. Cool; cut into bars.

Makes 24 bars

Rich Toffee Bars

A rich layer of toffee bits sandwiched between cookie layers loaded with chocolate chips and nuts. They are wonderful, wonderful, wonderful.

2⅓ cups	flour	550 mL
½ tsp.	salt	2 mL
⅔ cup	brown sugar	150 mL
¾ cup	butter OR margarine	175 mL
1	egg, lightly beaten	1
1 tsp.	vanilla	5 mL
2 cups	semisweet chocolate chips, divided	500 mL
1 cup	chopped pecans	250 mL
14 oz.	can sweetened condensed milk	396 g
1¾ cups	toffee bits, divided	425 mL

Preheat oven to 350°F (180°C). In a large bowl, combine flour, salt and brown sugar. With a pastry cutter or 2 knives, cut in butter until mixture resembles coarse crumbs. Stir in egg and vanilla. Stir in 1½ cups (375 mL) of the chocolate chips and the pecans. Set aside 1½ cups (375 mL) of the crumb mixture. Press remaining crumb mixture into the bottom of a lightly buttered 9 x 13" (23 x 33 cm) baking pan. Bake for 10 minutes. Remove from oven and pour condensed milk evenly over the hot crust; top with 1½ cups (375 mL) of the toffee bits. Sprinkle with reserved crumb mixture and the remaining chocolate chips. Return the pan to the oven; bake for 25-35 minutes, until golden brown. Remove pan from oven; immediately sprinkle the remaining toffee bits over top. Cool completely in the pan on a wire rack. Cut into small bars.

Makes 48 bars

Butterscotch and Chocolate Peanut Bars

These are yummy! A chocolate cookie base with a rich butterscotch and peanut topping.

1½ cups	flour	375 mL
½ cup	sugar	125 mL
¼ cup	firmly packed brown sugar	60 mL
½ tsp.	baking soda	2 mL
½ tsp.	salt	2 mL
½ cup	butter OR margarine, softened	125 mL
2 tbsp.	milk	30 mL
1	egg, lightly beaten	1
1 tsp.	vanilla	5 mL
1 cup	chocolate chips	250 mL

Butterscotch Peanut Topping:

¼ cup	corn syrup	60 mL
2 tbsp.	butter OR margarine	30 mL
1 tbsp.	milk	15 mL
2 cups	salted peanuts	500 mL
1 cup	butterscotch chips	250 mL

Preheat oven to 350°F (180°C). In a large bowl, combine flour, sugar, brown sugar, baking soda and salt; stir well. Add butter, milk, egg and vanilla; mix with an electric mixer at medium speed until dough is crumbly. Press into the bottom of an ungreased 9 x 13" (23 x 33 cm) baking pan. Bake for 15-20 minutes, or until golden brown. Remove from oven and sprinkle with chocolate chips; spreading the chocolate evenly over the base as the chips melt. Set aside.

Topping: In a medium saucepan, combine corn syrup, butter and milk. Place over medium heat and bring to a boil. Boil for 1 minute; remove from heat. Stir butterscotch chips and peanuts into the hot syrup. Cool slightly, then spread peanut batter over base. Cool completely and cut into bars. May be wrapped well and frozen for up to 2 months.

Makes 36 bars

Peanut Squares

For a quick sweet fix, make these easy squares at home or at the campsite.

3 cups	salted peanuts, divided	750 mL
3 tbsp.	butter OR margarine	45 mL
2 cups	peanut butter chips OR butterscotch chips	500 mL
14 oz.	can sweetened condensed milk	396 g
2 cups	miniature marshmallows	500 mL

Place half of the peanuts in an ungreased 9" (23 cm) square baking pan; set aside. In a saucepan, over low heat, melt butter and peanut butter chips. Add milk and marshmallows. Cook and stir until melted and well combined. Pour peanut mixture over peanuts. Sprinkle the remaining peanuts on top. Cover and refrigerate. Cut into squares.

Makes 48 squares

Peanut Butter Crunchies

These "no bake" squares are favorites of our sister-in-law Marion. She cuts them into bars and wraps them individually for picnics or trail rides. They are also great for school lunches.

5 cups	any dry cereal, not sugar coated	1.25 L
½ cup	shelled sunflower seeds	125 mL
½ cup	sesame seeds	125 mL
1 cup	liquid honey	250 mL
1 cup	crunchy peanut butter	250 mL

In a large bowl, combine cereal, sunflower seeds and sesame seeds. In a small saucepan, combine honey and peanut butter. Place over medium heat, stirring constantly, until mixture is hot, bubbly and thick. Remove from heat and immediately pour over the cereal mixture. Mix well to moisten cereal completely. Press the cereal mixture into a lightly buttered 9 x 13" (23 x 33 cm) baking pan. Cut into desired sizes and refrigerate to set.

Makes 32 squares or 16 bars

Marshmallow Peanut Squares

Marshmallow is sandwiched between a crisp cookie base and crunchy topping.

Cookie Crust:

1½ cups	flour	375 mL
⅔ cup	firmly packed brown sugar	150 mL
½ tsp.	baking powder	2 mL
½ tsp.	salt	2 mL
¼ tsp.	baking soda	1 mL
½ cup	butter OR margarine, softened	125 mL
1 tsp.	vanilla	5 mL
2	egg yolks	2
4 cups	miniature marshmallows	1 L

Peanut Topping:

⅔ cup	corn syrup	150 mL
¼ cup	butter OR margarine	60 mL
2 tsp.	vanilla	10 mL
2 cups	peanut butter chips OR chocolate chips	500 mL
2 cups	crisp rice cereal	500 mL
2 cups	salted peanuts	500 mL

Preheat oven to 350°F (180°C). In a large bowl, combine all crust ingredients, EXCEPT marshmallows. With an electric mixer, beat on low speed until crumbly. Press firmly into the bottom of a 9 x 13" (23 x 33 cm) baking pan. Bake for 12-15 minutes, or until light golden brown. Remove from oven and immediately sprinkle marshmallows over top. Return to oven and bake for an additional 1-2 minutes, or until marshmallows just begin to puff. Remove pan from oven and set aside to cool while preparing topping.

Topping: In a large saucepan, combine corn syrup, butter, vanilla and peanut butter chips. Place over low heat and cook, stirring constantly, until mixture is smooth. Remove from heat; stir in cereal and peanuts. Immediately spoon warm topping over marshmallows; spread to cover the base. Refrigerate until firm. Cut into squares.

Makes 36 squares

Aunt Susie's Date and Nut Cake with Caramel Coconut Frosting

1 cup	chopped dates	250 mL
1 cup	boiling water	250 mL
1 cup	sugar	250 mL
¼ cup	butter OR margarine, softened	60 mL
1	egg	1
1 tsp.	vanilla	5 mL
1½ cups	flour	375 mL
½ tsp.	baking soda	2 mL
1 tsp.	baking powder	5 mL
½ tsp.	salt	2 mL
½ cup	chopped walnuts OR pecans	125 mL

Caramel Coconut Frosting:

½ cup	brown sugar	125 mL
2 tbsp.	half-and-half cereal cream OR whipping cream	30 mL
2 tbsp.	butter OR margarine	30 mL
½ cup	coconut	125 mL

Preheat oven to 325°F (160°C). Place chopped dates in a large bowl; pour boiling water over and set aside to soften. When date mixture is cool, add sugar, butter, egg and vanilla. Beat until mixture is well combined. In a small bowl, combine flour, baking soda, baking powder and salt. Stir into the date mixture and mix well. Stir in nuts. Pour batter into a lightly buttered 9 x 13" (23 x 33 cm) baking pan, Bake for 45-55 minutes, or until a cake tester inserted in the center of the cake comes out clean.

Frosting: While the cake is baking, prepare frosting. In a small saucepan, combine brown sugar, cream and butter. Set over medium heat and bring to a boil, stirring constantly. When the cake is baked, remove from oven and pour frosting over the hot cake. Sprinkle with coconut and return to oven for 5-7 minutes to brown frosting.

Serves 12-15

Super Moist Chocolate Cake

This super moist, rich dark chocolate cake recipe was our Mother's favorite.

1½ cups	flour	375 mL
1 cup	sugar	250 mL
1 tsp.	baking powder	5 mL
1 tsp.	baking soda	5 mL
½ tsp.	salt	2 mL
3 tbsp.	cocoa powder	45 mL
1 cup	warm water	250 mL
5 tbsp.	vegetable oil	75 mL
1	egg	1
1 tbsp.	vinegar	15 mL
1 tsp.	vanilla	5 mL

Preheat oven to 350°F (180°C). In a large bowl, combine flour, sugar, baking powder, baking soda, salt and cocoa powder and mix well. Make a hole in the center and add warm water, vegetable oil, egg, vinegar and vanilla. Stir well to combine all ingredients. Pour batter into a lightly buttered 9 x 13" (23 x 33 cm) baking pan. Bake for 30-45 minutes, or until a cake tester, inserted in the center of the cake comes out clean. Ice with the Chocolate Icing below.

Serves 12-15

Creamy Chocolate Icing

¼ cup	butter OR margarine	60 mL
⅓ cup	cocoa powder	75 mL
½ cup	sour cream	125 mL
2¼ cups	icing (confectioner's) sugar	550 mL

Melt butter in a saucepan over low heat. Add cocoa powder, stirring constantly over low heat until smooth. Stir in sour cream; remove from heat. With an electric mixer, beat until smooth. Add ½ cup (125 mL) icing sugar; beat until smooth. Beat in remaining sugar slowly; blend well after each addition. Add additional icing sugar, if needed.

Makes 1⅔ cups (400 mL)

Sunday Brunch in the RV

Strawberry, Orange and Beef Salad, page 88
Cheddar Dill Muffins, page 11
Peach Shortcake, page 152
Red Wine Sangria with Peaches, page 60

Breakfast & Brunch
Picnics & Lunch

Savory Pies
Egg Dishes
Sandwiches
Pizzas

Apple and Sausage Bake

A real crowd pleaser, cornbread is baked on rows of brown-sugar-glazed apple slices and sausages. A great breakfast, brunch or lunch dish.

Sausage and Apple Upside Down Topping:

¾ lb.	breakfast pork sausages	340 g
¼ cup	butter OR margarine	60 mL
½ cup	brown sugar	125 mL
5	small apples, peeled, cut in eigths	5

Cornbread:

1 cup	flour	250 mL
1 cup	cornmeal	250 mL
¼ cup	brown sugar	60 mL
1 tbsp.	baking powder	15 mL
1 tsp.	salt	5 mL
2	eggs, lightly beaten	2
¼ cup	butter OR margarine, melted	60 mL
1 cup	milk	250 mL

Preheat oven to 400°F (200°C). In a skillet, brown sausages and cook through. Remove and set aside. Discard all but 2 tbsp. (30 mL) of drippings. Add butter and brown sugar to skillet. Heat, stirring constantly, until sugar is melted. Add apples and sauté over medium heat, stirring occasionally, until apples are soft, about 10 minutes. Arrange sausages across the bottom of a lightly buttered 9 x 13" (23 x 33 cm) baking dish. Insert apple wedges between rows of sausages, wedging them in tightly. Pour pan juices over; set aside.

Cornbread: In a large bowl, combine flour, cornmeal, brown sugar, baking powder and salt; stir well. Add egg, butter and milk; stir well. Pour batter over apples and sausages. Smooth top. Bake for 20 to 30 minutes, or until a cake tester inserted in the center comes out clean. Remove from oven and immediately invert onto a serving platter. Cut into squares and serve immediately with maple syrup.

Serves 6-8

Note: Sausages and apples may be cooked and refrigerated overnight.

Cheddar 'n' Corn, Sausage Pie

Hearty and satisfying, serve this for brunch or lunch with a green salad.

1 lb.	pork sausage links	500 g
1	green pepper, chopped	1
½ cup	chopped celery	125 mL
1 tbsp.	vegetable oil	15 mL
3 cups	cooked long-grain rice	750 mL
4	tomatoes, chopped	4
1½ cups	corn, canned or frozen and thawed	375 mL
1 cup	shredded Cheddar cheese	250 mL
1 tbsp.	Worcestershire sauce	15 mL
1 tsp.	salt	5 mL
1 tsp.	dried parsley	5 mL
1 tsp.	dried basil	5 mL
1 cup	soft bread crumbs	250 mL
2 tbsp.	butter OR margarine, melted	30 mL

Preheat oven to 350°F (180°C). Place sausages on a grilling rack and bake for 15 minutes, or until lightly browned. Remove from oven; cut into 1" (2.5 cm) pieces and set aside. In a small skillet, over medium heat, sauté pepper and celery in oil for 3 minutes, or until tender. In a lightly buttered 3-quart (3 L) casserole, combine the sausage chunks, sautéed pepper and celery, rice, tomatoes, corn, cheese, Worcestershire sauce, salt, parsley and basil; stir well. In a small bowl, combine the bread crumbs with the melted butter and sprinkle over the casserole. Bake, uncovered, for 30-45 minutes, or until heated through. Serve immediately.

Serves 6-8

🌲 **For a quick appetizer, brush hard or semi-hard cheeses, aged Cheddar, Edam, mozzarella, provolone, etc., with olive or canola oil, sprinkle with dried basil, oregano or mixed Italian spices and grill quickly to lightly brown the outside. Watch very carefully so that the cheese doesn't melt. Put cheese on foil if you are apprehensive about putting it directly on the grill. Serve with crackers, breads and/or fresh fruit.**

Scrambled Cheddar Dogs

1 tbsp.	butter OR margarine	15 mL
1	onion, thinly sliced	1
6	eggs	6
3 tbsp.	milk	45 mL
½ tsp.	salt	2 mL
½ cup	shredded Cheddar cheese	125 mL
4	hot dog buns, warmed	4

Heat butter in a frying pan. Add onions and cook until limp. In a small bowl, combine eggs, milk and salt; beat together until blended. Add eggs to onions in frying pan. Cook and stir over moderate heat. As eggs begin to set, gently stir up the bottom until eggs are set but still moist. Fold cheese into eggs. Pile eggs into warm hot dog rolls. Top with your favorite toppings (salsa, shredded cheese, ketchup, etc.).

Serves 4

Campfire Scrambled Eggs

6 slices	bacon, cooked crisp, crumbled	6 slices
½ cup	chopped onion	125 mL
12 oz.	can whole kernel corn	341 mL
4	eggs	4
½ cup	sour cream	125 mL
¼ tsp.	salt	1 mL
⅛ tsp.	pepper	0.5 mL
½ tsp.	Worcestershire sauce	2 mL

Over medium-hot campfire or grill, cook bacon. Remove bacon from pan. Pour off all but 2 tbsp. (30 mL) of drippings. Add onion and corn to pan and cook, stirring often, until slightly browned. Beat eggs with sour cream and seasonings. Pour into corn mixture in pan and scramble gently until eggs are firm, but still moist. Serve topped with crumbled bacon.

Serves 3-4

Pictured on page 17.

Mushroom Eggs with Hollandaise

Luxurious flavor but very easy to prepare.

2 tbsp.	butter OR margarine	30 mL
1 lb.	fresh mushrooms, sliced	500 g
¼ tsp.	salt	1 mL
⅛ tsp.	pepper	0.5 mL
8	slices toast	8
8	poached eggs	8
	Hollandaise Sauce, see below	

In a large frying pan, heat butter over medium-high heat. When hot add mushrooms and fry until tender and slightly browned. Add salt and pepper. Divide mushroom slices among 8 slices of toast. Top each portion with a poached egg and spoon on some Hollandaise Sauce. Serve immediately.

Serves 4

Hollandaise Sauce

½ cup	butter	125 mL
2	egg yolks	2
1 tsp.	lemon juice	5 mL
⅓ cup	boiling water	75 mL
dash	EACH salt, cayenne pepper	dash

Divide butter into thirds. Beat egg yolks with lemon juice in top of double boiler; add ⅓ of the butter. Place over simmering, not boiling water; cook, beating constantly, until butter melts and sauce starts to thicken; add remaining butter, half at a time, as above. Beat in boiling water slowly. Continue cooking and stirring, over simmering water, for 3 minutes, or until the sauce thickens; remove from water. Stir in salt and cayenne pepper.

Baked Egg Tomato Cups

We like to use basil; use your favorite herbs and/or a dash of hot pepper sauce.

4	tomatoes	4
4 tsp.	butter OR margarine	20 mL
	basil, fresh or dried	
4	eggs	4
¼ tsp.	salt	1 mL
⅛ tsp.	pepper	0.5 mL
¼ cup	Parmesan cheese	60 mL

Cut tomato tops across, like lids, but do not separate from the tomatoes. Spoon out the tomato pulp. Put 1 tsp. (5 mL) of butter and a dash of basil in each tomato. Break 1 egg into each tomato; season with salt, pepper and Parmesan cheese. Close the lid. Place tomatoes in a lightly greased heat-proof grilling pan or muffin tins; cover with foil. Grill over medium-hot, direct heat for 25-35 minutes.

Serves 4

Variation: Bake in the oven at 450°F (230°C) for 20-30 minutes.

Hawaiian Pizza

This pizza on a loaf is fast and easy.

1	loaf French Bread	1
1½ cups	pizza sauce	375 mL
½ cup	thinly sliced onions	125 mL
½ lb.	cooked ham, thinly sliced	250 g
1	green pepper, seeded, sliced	1
19 oz.	can pineapple tidbits, drained	540 g
½ lb.	fresh mushrooms, sliced	250 g
2 cups	shredded mozzarella cheese	500 mL

Cut bread in half lengthwise; spread with pizza sauce. On both halves, layer all remaining ingredients. Place loaf halves on a cookie sheet; broil 4" (10 cm) from heat until cheese melts.

Serves 6-8

Party Muffuletta

A version of the New Orleans' specialty, one of the world's great sandwiches.

Olive Salad:

¾ cup	olive oil	175 mL
10 oz.	jar pimiento-stuffed green olives, drained, coarsely chopped	285 g
20	Greek olives, pitted, coarsely chopped	20
3 tbsp.	vinegar	45 mL
3	garlic cloves, minced	3
1 tsp.	dried parsley leaves	5 mL
½ tsp.	dried oregano leaves	2 mL
1	10" (25 cm) loaf round crusty Italian OR sourdough bread	1
½ lb.	cooked ham, thinly sliced	250 g
½ lb.	roast turkey breast, thinly sliced	250 g
10	lettuce leaves	10
4	tomatoes, sliced	4
½ lb.	salami, thinly sliced	250 g
½ lb.	mozzarella cheese slices	250 g
8-12	8" (20 cm) long wooden skewers	8-12

Combine all olive salad ingredients; cover and refrigerate.

With a bread knife, cut bread horizontally 3 times, creating 4 layers of equal thickness. With a pastry brush, lightly coat cut sides of bread layers with dressing from olive salad. Place bottom bread layer on cutting board, cut side up. Arrange ham, turkey, 6 lettuce leaves and tomato on bread. Place the second bread layer on top. Spoon olive salad over bread and spread to edge; top with the third bread layer. Arrange salami, cheese and the remaining lettuce leaves on bread layer. Top with the last bread layer, cut side down. Skewer with 4 rows of 3 skewers, equally spaced. Refrigerate until ready to serve. Just before serving, cut between skewers to make 8-12 kabobs.

Serves 12

Pictured on page 103.

Turkey 'n' Corned Beef Party Animals

A complete meal in a loaf, this easy muffuletta-style recipe is easy to serve and oh-so-impressive.

¾ lb.	creamy coleslaw	340 g
⅓ cup	bottled creamy Italian or creamy blue cheese salad dressing	75 mL
1	loaf round Italian, rye, OR sourdough bread	1
8-10	lettuce leaves	8-10
½ lb.	cooked turkey, thinly sliced	250 g
½ lb.	cooked corned beef, thinly sliced	250 g
¼ lb.	Swiss cheese, sliced	125 g

Drain excess liquid from coleslaw; add 2 tbsp. (30 mL) bottled dressing to coleslaw, mixing well. Cut a thin slice from top of bread; spread cut surface of the slice with some of the bottled dressing. Hollow out the bread, leaving a 1½" (4 cm) thick bread shell. Line shell with lettuce; brush with remaining bottled dressing. Press turkey over bottom of loaf; cover with half of coleslaw mixture. Repeat with corned beef, remaining coleslaw mixture and cheese. Garnish with lettuce; cover with the bread lid. Place 6-8 long wooden picks into the sandwich to secure. Chill 4 hours before serving, but no longer than 6 hours. To serve, cut between the picks to form 6-8 wedge-shaped sandwiches.
Serves 6-8

BBQ Beef Sandwiches

Great flavor for the second time around.

1 cup	barbecue sauce	250 mL
1 tbsp.	cider vinegar	15 mL
2 tsp.	prepared mustard	10 mL
1 tbsp.	Worcestershire sauce	15 mL
1 lb.	cooked roast beef, thinly sliced	500 g
1	small red onion, thinly sliced	1
4	hamburger buns or Kaiser buns, toasted	4

BB2 Beef Sandwiches Continued

In a small saucepan, combine barbecue sauce, vinegar, mustard and Worcestershire sauce. Place over medium-high heat and bring to a boil; reduce heat and simmer for 2 minutes. Toast buns; fill with beef slices, onion slices and top with sauce. Garnish with dill pickles.

Serves 4

Variation: Substitute cooked ham for roast beef.

Monte Cristo Tuna Sandwiches

Give your tuna sandwich a new twist.

6½ oz.	can tuna, drained and flaked	184 g
½ cup	chopped celery	125 mL
2	chopped green onions	2
¼ cup	chopped green grapes	60 mL
¼ cup	mayonnaise	60 mL
2 tsp.	prepared mustard	10 mL
¼ tsp.	salt	1 mL
⅛ tsp.	pepper	0.5 mL
8 slices	bread	8 slices
2	eggs	2
¼ cup	milk	60 mL
2 tbsp.	butter OR margarine	30 mL

In a medium bowl, combine tuna, celery, onions, grapes, mayonnaise, mustard, salt and pepper. Stir well and spread on 4 slices of bread. Top with remaining bread slices. In a wide shallow bowl, beat together eggs and milk. Dip sandwiches into egg mixture, moistening both sides. In a skillet, over medium-high heat, melt butter and fry sandwiches until golden brown and crisp on both sides. Serve immediately.

Serves 4

Ham and Cheese Biscuit Pockets

1 cup	cubed cooked ham	250 mL
1 cup	shredded Swiss cheese	250 mL
½ cup	finely chopped, peeled apple	125 mL
10 oz.	refrigerator biscuits	285 g
1	egg, lightly beaten	1
1 tsp.	water	5 mL

Preheat oven to 350°F (190°C). In a small bowl, combine ham, cheese and apple. Separate dough into 10 biscuits. On a lightly buttered cookie sheet, press out 5 biscuits into 4" (10 cm) circles. Place about ½ cup (125 mL) of ham mixture in the center of each circle. Press out remaining 5 biscuits to 5" (13 cm) circles. Place 1 over each filled biscuit. Press edges with a fork to seal. Combine egg and water; brush over filled biscuits. Bake for 15-20 minutes, or until golden brown. Remove pockets from oven; allow to sit 5 minutes on cookie sheet. Cut each in half to form pocket sandwiches. To serve, garnish with alfalfa sprouts and tomatoes. Serve warm. To reheat, wrap loosely in foil and place in 350°F (180°C) oven for 12-15 minutes, or place on grill for 8-10 minutes.

Serves 5

Variation: **Roast Beef Biscuit Sandwich** – **In a bowl, combine ½ cup (125 mL) chopped, cooked or deli-style roast beef, ¼ cup (60 mL) taco sauce, ¼ cup (60 mL) barbecue sauce, ¼ cup (60 mL) sliced green onions, ¼ cup (60 mL) sliced olives, drained, ½ cup (125 mL) shredded Cheddar cheese**. Prepare as above with refrigerator biscuits. Using the back of a tablespoon, make an indentation in the center of each sandwich. Sprinkle sandwiches with **1 tbsp. (15 mL) of cornmeal**. Bake as above. Remove sandwiches from oven; transfer to serving plates and fill each center with a **heaping tablespoon (22 mL) of sour cream**. Garnish with additional sliced olives or pimiento slices.

Variation: Instead of the refrigerator biscuits, you can use the Basic Biscuit Mix, page 9. Use the 2-cup (500 mL) recipe and divide dough into 10 biscuits.

Bacon Tomato Open-Faced Rounds

A new twist for the ever popular BLT.

10 oz.	can refrigerator biscuits	258 g
10 slices	bacon, cut into thirds, crisply cooked	10 slices
10 slices	tomato	10 slices
½ cup	mayonnaise	125 mL
½ cup	chopped onion	125 mL
½ cup	shredded Swiss cheese	125 mL
1 tsp.	dried basil	5 mL

Preheat oven to 400°F (200°C). Separate dough into 10 biscuits. On an ungreased cookie sheet, press out each biscuit to a 4" (10 cm) circle, forming a rim around the edge of each circle. Arrange 3 bacon pieces on each circle; top each with a tomato slice. In a small bowl, combine mayonnaise, onion, cheese and basil. Spoon a rounded tablespoonful (22 mL) of the mayonnaise mixture over each tomato slice, spreading slightly. Bake for 10-15 minutes, or until edges of biscuits are golden brown. Serve immediately. To reheat, wrap loosely in foil; heat at 350°F (180°C) for 15-20 minutes, until warm, or warm over a grill or campfire.

Makes 10 sandwiches

Variation: Instead of the refrigerator biscuits, you can use the Basic Biscuit Mix, page 9. Use the 2-cup (500 mL) recipe and divide dough into 10 biscuits.

When possible, take meat items frozen.

Corn Dogs with Honey Mustard Sauce

Who can resist corn dogs when they are served with this sweet and tangy sauce!

Corn Dogs:

1 cup	flour	250 mL
1 cup	cornmeal	250 mL
1 tbsp.	baking powder	15 mL
1 tsp.	salt	5 mL
¼ cup	butter OR margarine	60 mL
¾ cup	milk	175 mL
6	wieners OR smokies	6

Preheat oven to 425°F (220°C). In a large bowl, combine flour, cornmeal, baking powder and salt; stir well. With pastry blender or 2 knives, cut in butter until mixture resembles coarse crumbs. Add milk, stirring only until mixture forms a soft dough that leaves the sides of the bowl. Turn dough onto a lightly floured surface; knead gently to mix thoroughly. Pat or roll dough into a 9 x 13" (23 x 33 cm) rectangle. Cut dough into 6 equal portions and place a wiener on each portion. Bring sides of dough up and around wiener; pinch a seam in the center to seal. Repeat with the remaining 5 wieners. Place wrapped wieners, seam side down, on an ungreased cookie sheet. Bake for 10-12 minutes, or until golden brown. Serve immediately with Honey Mustard Sauce.

Serves 6

Honey Mustard Sauce

⅓ cup	liquid honey	75 mL
⅓ cup	prepared mustard	75 mL
6 drops	hot pepper sauce	6 drops

In a small bowl, combine all sauce ingredients. Stir well.

Makes ⅔ cup (150 mL)

Beef Stroganoff Sandwich

An old favorite on a loaf – portable and delicious.

2 lbs.	lean ground beef	1 kg
½ cup	chopped onion	125 mL
3	garlic cloves, minced	3
2 tsp.	Worcestershire sauce	10 mL
1 tsp.	salt	5 mL
½ tsp.	pepper	2 mL
1 loaf	French bread	1 loaf
	butter OR margarine, softened	
2 cups	sour cream	500 mL
2	tomatoes, diced	2
1	green pepper, diced	1
3 cups	shredded Cheddar cheese	750 mL

Preheat oven to 350°F (180°C). In a large skillet, over medium-high heat, combine ground beef, onion and garlic. Cook, stirring often, until meat is browned and no pink shows through. Drain off all fat and add Worcestershire sauce, salt and pepper; stir to combine. Cut bread lengthwise in half; hollow out the bread, leaving 2" (5 cm) thick bread shells. Butter the inside of both halves and place on a baking sheet. Remove the meat mixture from the heat; stir in sour cream. Spoon meat mixture onto the bread. Sprinkle with tomatoes, green pepper and cheese. Bake for 20-30 minutes, or until cheese is melted. Cut into wedges and serve immediately.

Serves 8-10

Make freezer packs by filling heavy zip-top plastic bags three-quarters full with water; seal and lay flat in freezer. These are wonderful in a cooler.

Beef 'n' Garlic Cabbage Buns

This recipe comes from Jo's auction sale buddy, Audrey Bensmiller, who always takes these buns on their long cattle drives. They are easy to pack and delicious.

Beef 'n' Garlic Filling:

1	small head cabbage, shredded	1
1 tsp.	salt	5 mL
¼ tsp.	pepper	1 mL
¼ cup	vinegar	60 mL
2-3 cups	water	500-750 mL
1 lb.	lean ground beef	500 g
2	garlic cloves, minced	2
1 tsp.	salt	5 mL
¼ tsp.	pepper	1 mL

Bun Dough:

6 cups	lukewarm water	1.5 L
⅓ cup	butter OR margarine, melted	75 mL
2 tsp.	salt	10 mL
¼ cup	sugar	60 mL
12 cups	flour	2.8 L
2 tbsp.	active dry yeast	30 mL

Beef 'n' Garlic Filling: In a large saucepan, combine cabbage, salt, pepper, vinegar and water; cover and place over medium heat; boil until tender. Drain well and place in a strainer to cool. In a large frying pan, combine ground beef, garlic, salt and pepper. Over medium-high heat, cook until meat is browned and no pink shows through. Add meat mixture to cabbage in strainer to drain off fat and moisture. Cool. Cabbage/meat mixture can be made up the night before and stored in the refrigerator.

Beef 'n' Garlic Cabbage Buns Continued

Bun Dough: In a large bowl, combine lukewarm water, melted butter, salt and sugar; stir well. Add 6 cups (1.4 L) of the flour; sprinkle with the 2 tbsp. (30 mL) of yeast; mix well. Add enough remaining flour to make a soft dough, not sticky. Knead well for 5 to 10 minutes. Let rise for 20 minutes; knead again. Do this 3 times. After the third rising, make into buns.

Pinch off 2-3 tbsp. (30-45 mL) of dough (or enough dough for the size of bun you may want). Flatten the dough and place 1 tbsp. (15 mL) of cabbage/meat mixture in the center of the bun; pull up dough around the mixture; pinch tightly to form a bun. Place buns on lightly buttered cookie sheets, seam down. Cover with a clean tea towel. Let buns rise for 1 hour in a warm place, free from drafts.

Preheat oven to 400°F (200°C). Bake for 25-35 minutes, or until nicely browned.

Note: Buns can be made any size or shape. They can be eaten warm or cold and are wonderful warmed up over the campfire. Buns may be wrapped well and frozen for up to 1 month.

Variations:

🌲 1 cup (250 mL) of cooked rice may be added to the cabbage and meat mixture.

🌲 A variety of different spices may be added – rosemary, sage, chili.

🌲 Barbecue sauce or soy sauce may also be added.

🌲 For a quick and easy version, the cabbage/meat mixture is also very tasty served warm in a pita.

Spinach and Salmon Roulade

This is a spectacular must-try recipe. Roulade crust is similar to soufflé crust. It is delicious when spread with any filling and rolled up jelly-roll style. We have chosen some of our favorite fillings. Serve hot or cold.

Spinach Crust:

10 oz.	pkg. frozen chopped spinach	285 g
4	eggs, separated	4
½ cup	butter OR margarine	125 mL
⅓ cup	flour	75 mL
1 cup	milk	250 mL
½ tsp.	salt	2 mL
½ tsp.	hot pepper sauce	2 mL
½ tsp.	Worcestershire sauce	2 mL
2 tbsp.	Parmesan cheese	30 mL
2 tbsp.	bread crumbs	30 mL

Salmon Filling:

2 x 7 oz.	cans red salmon, drained, flaked	2 x 200 g
4	green onions, chopped	4
½ cup	mayonnaise	125 mL

Crust: Preheat oven to 425°F (220°C). Place frozen spinach in a small saucepan; cook over medium heat until all liquid has evaporated. Squeeze dry and set aside. Beat egg whites until soft peaks form; set aside. In a separate bowl, lightly beat egg yolks and set aside. In a saucepan over medium heat, melt butter; add flour and cook, stirring constantly, for 1 minute. Add milk gradually, cook and stir until mixture boils and thickens. Remove from heat and quickly stir in egg yolks, spinach, salt, hot pepper sauce and Worcestershire sauce; mix well. Gently fold in beaten egg whites; combine well. Lightly butter a 10 x 15" (25 x 38 cm) baking pan; line with well-buttered waxed paper. Pour batter into prepared pan and bake for 15-20 minutes, or until puffed and golden brown and center feels firm when gently pressed.

Filling: In a small bowl, combine all filling ingredients; mix well.

Spinach and Salmon Roulade Continued

Remove crust from oven; dust top with combined Parmesan cheese and bread crumbs. Place a tea towel on top and gently invert onto a work surface. Carefully remove lining paper. Spread filling evenly over crust. Gently roll up the long side in jelly-roll fashion. Serve immediately. Roulades can be prepared several hours ahead, wrapped in foil, refrigerated and reheated at 350°F (180°C) for 15-20 minutes.

Serves 4-5

Crust Variations:

Cheese Crust: Omit the spinach; add ¾ cup (175 mL) grated Cheddar cheese and prepare as above.

Tomato Crust: Omit the spinach; use ½ cup (125 mL) of flour instead of ⅓ cup (75 mL); add 2 tbsp. (30 mL) of tomato paste and prepare as above.

Filling Variations:

Crab Filling: Substitute crab for salmon; add ¼ cup (60 mL) finely chopped celery; ½ tsp. (2 mL) dillweed and prepare as above.

Corn and Bacon Filling: In a saucepan or frying pan, cook 10 slices of bacon until crisp then crumble. Combine the bacon with a 14 oz. (398 mL) can of corn. Heat to boiling over medium heat. Combine 1 tsp. (5 mL) of cornstarch and 2 tsp. (10 mL) of water; add to the corn mixture; stir and cook until mixture boils and thickens. Remove from heat and stir in 2 tbsp. (30 mL) of sour cream, ¼ cup (60 mL) of chopped, green onions and 6-8 drops of hot pepper sauce. Spread over roulade crust and proceed as above.

Pizza in a Loaf

A meal in a dish, this is great for picnics or camping trips. Serve hot or cold.

Dough:

1 tbsp.	active dry yeast (7 g env.)	15 mL
1 tsp.	sugar	5 mL
¾ cup	lukewarm water	175 mL
2 cups	flour	500 mL

Pizza Filling:

1 cup	shredded mozzarella cheese	250 mL
½ lb.	salami, sliced	250 g
½ cup	tomato sauce	125 mL
½ tsp.	dried oregano	2 mL
1 lb.	broccoli, in small florets	500 g
1	egg, lightly beaten	1
1	red pepper, seeded, sliced	1
½ lb.	pepperoni, thinly sliced	250 g
1 cup	stuffed green olives, halved lengthwise	250 mL

Dough: Preheat oven to 350°F (180°C). Pour water into a small bowl; add sugar and stir until dissolved. Sprinkle yeast over top. Do not stir. Let stand 10-15 minutes, until foamy on top. Measure flour into a large mixing bowl. When yeast is foamy, stir down with a fork; make a well in flour and add yeast. Mix to form a firm dough. Transfer to a floured surface; knead 5-8 minutes, until dough is smooth and elastic. Using ¾ of the dough, roll out to a rectangle to line a well-buttered 5 x 9" (13 x 23 cm) loaf pan; leaving approximately 1" (2.5 cm) of dough over edge.

Filling: Sprinkle mozzarella evenly over dough; top with rolled up salami slices. Combine tomato sauce and oregano; pour over salami. Arrange broccoli over tomato sauce. Pour over beaten egg. Add a layer of red peppers. Arrange pepperoni then olives over peppers.

Roll out remaining dough to cover loaf. Place dough on top; pinch edges to seal; use a little water if necessary. Cut slits in top crust for steam to escape. Bake for 40-50 minutes. Remove loaf from pan; place on a cookie sheet; bake for 10 minutes to brown sides. Cover the top with foil if it is getting too brown. Cool before cutting or refrigerate if serving later. Serves 6-8

Drinks & Appetizers

Punches

Shakes

Sangrias

Dips

Spreads

Lemon-Lime Concentrate

A real thirst quencher on a hot day – keep this handy concentrate on hand for old-fashioned fruit flavor.

1½ cups	sugar	375 mL
1½ cups	water	375 mL
1 tbsp.	grated lemon rind	15 mL
1 cup	fresh lemon juice	250 mL
¾ cup	fresh lime juice	175 mL

In a small saucepan, combine sugar, water and lemon rind; place over medium heat and bring to a boil, stirring occasionally. Boil for 5 minutes, stirring occasionally. Remove from heat and let cool. Stir in strained lemon and lime juice. Transfer concentrate to a jar with a tight-fitting lid. Refrigerate for at least 6 hours, or until chilled. Concentrate may be stored in refrigerator for up to 2 weeks.

To serve: add ¼ cup (60 mL) of concentrate to ¾ cup (175 mL) of cold water. Combine in a tall glass; stir well. Add ice cubes.

Makes 4 cups (1 L) of concentrate

Cran Pineapple Punch

Tart and refreshing.

3 cups	pineapple juice	750 mL
3 cups	cranberry juice	750 mL
3 cups	ginger ale or lemon-lime soda	750 mL
	lemon slices for garnish	

In a large pitcher, mix juices and soda; stir to combine. Pour over crushed ice in tall glasses. Garnish with lemon slices.

Serves 9

Pictured on page 121.

Chilled Apple Tea

Apple and lemon give a refreshing lift to iced tea.

6	regular tea bags	6
3 cups	freshly boiling water	750 mL
4 cups	apple juice	1 L
2 tbsp.	lemon juice	30 mL
	sugar	
	ice cubes	
	lemon wedges for garnish	

Place tea bags in a teapot or heat-proof container; pour in freshly boiling water. Brew 3-5 minutes; remove tea bags. Allow tea to cool to room temperature; pour into a large serving pitcher. Stir in apple juice, lemon juice and sugar to taste, if desired. Pour over ice cubes in tall glasses. Garnish with a lemon wedge.

Serves 8

Purple Cow

Everyone loves this drink.

2 cups	milk	500 mL
1 cup	grape juice	250 mL
2 cups	vanilla ice cream	500 mL

In a blender, combine milk, grape juice and 1 cup (250 mL) of the ice cream. Whirl at high speed until thick and foamy. Pour into 4 tall glasses. Top with remaining ice cream, divided evenly.

Serves 4

Variation: To make a **Pink Cow** – substitute cranberry or raspberry juice for grape.

Chocolate Lovers' Chocolate Syrup

Keep a supply in the fridge all year round. This appeals to everyone – young and old.

1½ cups	cocoa powder	375 mL
1½ cups	sugar	375 mL
2 cups	water	500 mL
2 tsp.	vanilla	10 mL

In a small saucepan, combine cocoa powder and sugar. Add water and stir well. Set over medium heat; cook, stirring constantly, until mixture comes to a boil. Reduce heat to low; boil gently for 5 minutes, stirring occasionally. Remove from heat and cool. Stir in vanilla. Cover and store in refrigerator.

To serve: Stir 3-4 tbsp. (45-60 mL) of Chocolate Syrup into hot or cold milk. It also makes a wonderful topping for ice cream, fruit, or cake.

Makes 3½ cups (875 mL)

Chocolate Banana Shake

1 cup	milk	250 mL
¼ cup	chocolate syrup (recipe above)	60 mL
1	medium banana, peeled and quartered	1
2 scoops	vanilla ice cream	2 scoops

Place all ingredients in a blender or a food processor with the steel blade attachment. Cover and blend until smooth. Serve immediately.

Serves 2

Variation: For a *Peanut Chocolate Shake* substitute ¼ cup (60 mL) peanut butter for the banana and prepare as above.

Peach Champagne Cocktail

This is truly an elegant drink, in both presentation and flavor.

2	fresh peaches, sliced	2
¼ cup	sugar	60 mL
26 oz.	pink champagne, chilled	750 mL

Roll peach slices in sugar and place 2-3 slices in each of 4 glasses. Fill with champagne.

Serves 4

Variation: This can also be a fruit starter for a Sunday Brunch; just fill champagne glasses with peach slices and top with champagne.

Sangria Blush

The orange juice gives this drink a wonderful color as well as flavor.

1 cup	orange juice	250 mL
½ cup	sugar	125 mL
26 oz.	dry white wine	750 mL
¼ cup	lime juice	60 mL
¼ cup	lemon juice	60 mL
1	orange, thinly sliced and seeded	1
1	lime, thinly sliced and seeded	1
	ice	

Combine orange juice and sugar in a small saucepan. Place over medium heat and cook, stirring occasionally, until sugar is dissolved. Pour juice into a 2-quart (2 L) container with a tight fitting lid. Add wine, lime juice, lemon juice and fruit slices. Cover and refrigerate for 2 hours for flavors to blend.

To serve: place ice in a large pitcher; pour wine mixture over ice.

Serves 8

Pictured on the back cover.

Red Wine Sangria with Peaches

This recipe comes from friends in California. They serve this sangria at brunches – it's very refreshing on a hot day.

¾ cup	sugar	175 mL
¾ cup	orange juice	175 mL
⅓ cup	lemon juice	75 mL
⅓ cup	lime juice	75 mL
2 x 26 oz.	medium dry red wine, chilled	2 x 750 mL
2	oranges, thinly sliced and seeded	2
2	peaches, thinly sliced	2
	ice cubes	

In a large pitcher, combine sugar and juices; stir until sugar dissolves. Cover and chill. Just before serving, add wine and fruit. Serve over ice.

Makes 2-quarts (2 L)

Variation: For *Sangria Slush*, omit fruit and ice. Combine sugar, juices and wine; stir well. Pour into a freezer container; cover and freeze for 8 hours or overnight.

Pictured on page 35.

Purple Passion

Good! Good! Good!

12½ oz.	can frozen grape juice concentrate, thawed	355 mL
3 x 12½ oz.	juice cans cold water	3 x 355 mL
12½ oz.	juice can vodka	355 mL
1 cup	fresh lemon juice	250 mL
½ cup	sugar	125 mL
	grapes for garnish (optional)	

In a large pitcher, combine all ingredients; stir until sugar dissolves. Cover and chill. Serve over ice and garnish with grapes, if desired.

Makes 2 quarts (2 L)

Citrus Slush

Jo serves her special slush combination on those hot Rocky Mountain summer days.

1 cup	sugar	250 mL
1 cup	boiling water	250 mL
6 cups	cold water	1.5 L
12½ oz.	can frozen orange juice concentrate	355 mL
12½ oz.	can frozen lemonade concentrate	355 mL
26 oz.	vodka or gin	750 mL

In a large freezer container, combine sugar and hot water; stir until sugar is dissolved. Add all remaining ingredients; stir well. Place in freezer and stir occasionally. To serve, place slush in tall glasses and add additional orange juice or soda, if desired.

Makes 4 quarts (4 L)

Cran Orange Slush

4 cups	cranberry juice cocktail	1 L
12½ oz.	can frozen orange juice concentrate, thawed	355 mL
2 cups	vodka	500 mL
12½ oz.	can frozen lemonade concentrate, thawed	355 mL

Combine all ingredients in a large freezer container; mix well and freeze. To serve, spoon frozen slush into goblets; add additional juice or soda, if desired.

Makes 2½ quarts (2.5 L)

Pictured on page 103.

Hot Spiced Cranberry Lemon Punch

A great hot drink on those cool rainy days, summer or winter.

2 x 12½ oz.	cans frozen lemonade concentrate, thawed	2 x 355 mL
4 cups	cranberry juice cocktail	1 L
½ tsp.	EACH salt, cinnamon and allspice	2 mL
2½ cups	water	625 mL

In a large saucepan, combine lemonade, cranberry juice, salt, cinnamon, allspice and water. Place over low heat and simmer, uncovered, for 10-15 minutes, do not boil. Serve hot.

Makes 12, 8 oz. (250 mL) servings

Eskimo Coffee

Quick, easy and delicious – it always tastes like more, especially when you're sitting around a campfire.

4 mugs	hot, strong black coffee	4 mugs
4 oz.	Canadian whiskey of your choice	120 mL
4 scoops	vanilla ice cream	4 scoops

Fill 4 mugs ¾ full with hot coffee. Add 1 oz. (30 mL) whiskey to each mug and top with a generous scoop of ice cream. Let the ice cream start to melt gently into the hot coffee before sipping.

Serves 4

For quick and easy, no-mess deviled eggs, slice hard-boiled eggs in half, put yolks, mayonnaise and seasonings in a plastic sandwich bag. Mash thoroughly in sealed bag; cut off a small corner of the bag and pipe the filling into the egg whites. This also works well for stuffed tomatoes.

Mexican Deviled Eggs

A super appetizer, picnic or barbecue side dish.

8	hard-cooked eggs, peeled	8
½ cup	shredded Cheddar cheese	125 mL
¼ cup	EACH mayonnaise and salsa	60 mL
2 tbsp.	sliced green onions	30 mL
1 tbsp.	sour cream	15 mL
¼ tsp.	salt	1 mL
⅛ tsp.	pepper	0.5 mL

Slice eggs in half lengthwise; remove yolks; set whites aside. In a small bowl, mash yolks with cheese, mayonnaise, salsa, onions, sour cream, salt and pepper. Mix well. Evenly fill the egg whites with the deviled yolk mixture. Serve immediately or refrigerate until ready to serve.

Serves 8

Pictured on the back cover.

Stuffed Cherry Tomatoes

Serve as an appetizer or a side dish. These are delicious and colorful.

12 oz.	cream cheese, softened	340 g
¼ cup	mayonnaise	60 mL
1 oz.	pkg. Ranch dressing mix	30 g
36	cherry tomatoes	36
	alfalfa sprouts	

Combine cream cheese, mayonnaise and dressing mix. Beat until smooth. Slice a thin slice off the top of each tomato and carefully remove the insides. Invert tomatoes on paper towel to drain. Fill tomatoes with cream cheese mixture. Serve on a bed of alfalfa sprouts.

Serves 10-12

Variation: Cheddar Cherry Tomatoes, decrease cream cheese to 8 oz. (250 g), omit Ranch dressing and add 1 cup (250 mL) shredded Cheddar cheese, ¼ tsp. (1 mL) cayenne pepper and 1 garlic clove, minced.

Pictured on the back cover.

Poppy Seed Fruited Cheese Roll

Serve this cream cheese fruit spread with fresh fruit and crackers.

½ cup	chopped mixed dried fruits	125 mL
¼ cup	chopped mixed candied fruits	60 mL
2 tbsp.	orange juice	30 mL
8 oz.	cream cheese, softened	250 g
½ cup	grated Cheddar cheese	125 mL
1 tsp.	grated orange rind	5 mL
¾ cup	poppy seeds	175 mL

In a small bowl, combine dried fruit, candied fruit and orange juice; stir well. Cover and allow to stand for 2 hours. In a large bowl, beat together cream cheese and Cheddar cheese; stir in orange rind and fruit mixture; mix well. Cover and refrigerate for 1 hour. Roll cheese mixture into a log shape approximately 8" (20 cm) in length; roll in poppy seeds. Wrap the cheese roll in waxed paper and refrigerate for 24 hours. Roll will keep in the refrigerator for up to 4 days.

Serves 10-12

Salmon Pâté in a Loaf

An elegant appetizer or lunch presentation, take it on that special picnic.

1 loaf	round Italian, French, OR sourdough bread	1 loaf
1 tbsp.	unflavored gelatin (7 g env.)	15 mL
⅓ cup	cold water	75 mL
8 oz.	cream cheese	250 g
2 x 7 oz.	cans red sockeye salmon, drained, flaked	2 x 200 g
¼ cup	mayonnaise	60 mL
1 tsp.	lemon juice	5 mL
3 tbsp.	chopped pimiento	45 mL
2 tbsp.	chopped onion	30 mL
¼ cup	finely chopped celery	60 mL
¼ cup	chopped dill pickles	60 mL
6-8 drops	hot pepper sauce	6-8 drops

Salmon Pâté in a Loaf Continued

With a sharp knife, carefully cut off the top crust of the bread, keeping it intact so it can be replaced over the filling. Carefully remove the center of the loaf, so that only a 1" (2.5 cm) shell of crust remains. Set aside.

In a small saucepan, soften gelatin in cold water; place over low heat and stir until gelatin is dissolved. Set aside to cool. In a large bowl, beat cream cheese; add flaked salmon and mix well. Gradually stir in dissolved gelatin. Add all remaining ingredients, mixing well. Pour salmon pâté into hollowed out bread round; cover with the top crust. Wrap in waxed paper and refrigerate for 8-10 hours, or overnight. To serve, slice in ½" (1.3 cm) slices or wedges.

Serves 8-10

Parmesan Garlic Dip

Super with fresh vegetables or with hot, spicy chicken wings or drumsticks.

⅔ cup	sour cream	150 mL
⅓ cup	mayonnaise	75 mL
½ cup	grated Parmesan cheese	125 mL
1 tbsp.	lemon juice	15 mL
3	garlic cloves, minced	3
6-8 drops	hot pepper sauce	6-8 drops

In a small bowl, combine all ingredients. Cover and refrigerate for 4 hours before serving.

Makes 1¼ cups (300 mL)

Roasted Garlic Chickpea Dip (Hummus)

"Tahini Paste" is made from ground sesame seeds and is available in health food, bulk and natural food stores, or in the Greek or Middle Eastern section of super markets.*

4	garlic cloves, roasted	4
19 oz.	can chickpeas, drained	540 mL
½ cup	tahini paste*	125 mL
½ cup	fresh lemon juice (approximately 2-3 lemons)	125 mL
½ tsp.	salt	2 mL
1 tbsp.	vegetable oil	15 mL
½ tsp.	ground paprika	2 mL
1 tbsp.	chopped fresh parsley, optional	15 mL

Preheat oven to 350°F (180°C). Place unpeeled garlic cloves in a garlic roaster or wrap garlic in foil and place on a cookie sheet; roast for 45-60 minutes. Squeeze roasted garlic cloves out of the peel into a blender or food processor fitted with a steel blade; add drained chickpeas, tahini paste, lemon juice, salt, oil and paprika. Process until mixture is puréed and smooth. Taste and adjust seasoning as desired. Transfer hummus to a serving dish and sprinkle with chopped parsley, if desired. This dip may be made ahead of time and refrigerated, or may be frozen for longer storage. Serve with pita bread or crackers.

Makes 2½ cups (625 mL)

Variations: In a pinch, substitute peanut butter* for the tahini paste. Add less to start and add more, as you prefer, for desired flavor. You may also add a dash of cayenne for a zestier dip.

Tzatziki

This classic, creamy Middle-Eastern cucumber dip will win you accolades.

1 cup	mayonnaise	250 mL
1 cup	plain yogurt OR sour cream*	250 mL
½ cup	cucumber, peeled, seeded and finely chopped	125 mL
2	garlic cloves, minced	2
1	green onion, finely chopped	1
1 tbsp.	lemon juice	15 mL
3 tbsp.	chopped fresh dill, or 1 tbsp. (15 mL) dried dill	45 mL .

In a large bowl, combine all ingredients. Refrigerate several hours or overnight. Serve with a variety of fresh vegetables and/or grilled pita.

Makes 2½ cups (625 mL)

* Use low-fat yogurt or sour cream if you prefer.

Layered Greek Dip

This easy-to-make layered spread is like a Greek salad on a cracker.

8 oz.	cream cheese, softened	250 g
½ cup	mayonnaise	125 mL
1 cup	chopped tomatoes	250 mL
1 cup	chopped, peeled, seeded cucumber	250 mL
1 cup	sliced black Greek olives	250 mL
¼ cup	chopped red onion	60 mL
½ cup	chopped green pepper	125 mL
½ cup	crumbled feta cheese	125 mL

In a small bowl, beat cream cheese and mayonnaise until well blended. Spread cheese mixture evenly over a 9" (23 cm) plate or serving platter. Top with tomatoes, cucumber, olives, red onion and green pepper. Sprinkle feta cheese over top. Serve with grilled pita bread or crackers.

Serves 6-8

Pictured on the back cover.

Zesty Bean Appetizer Flan

Zesty bean filling on top of a chili cornmeal biscuit crust, topped with cheese, olives, onions and peppers. A bit of a production to make, this is worth it.

Chili Cornmeal Crust:

1 ½ cups	flour	375 mL
½ cup	cornmeal	125 mL
2 tsp.	chili powder	10 mL
1½ tsp.	ground cumin	7 mL
½ tsp.	salt	2 mL
¾ cup	butter OR margarine	175 mL
⅓ cup	cold water	75 mL

Zesty Bean Filling:

19 oz.	can garbanzo beans, drained, rinsed	540 mL
½ cup	salsa	125 mL
¼ cup	chopped green onions	60 mL
2	garlic cloves, minced	2
¼ cup	sour cream	60 mL
2 tbsp.	lemon juice	30 mL
¼ tsp.	salt	1 mL
⅛ tsp.	pepper	0.5 mL

Topping:

½ cup	chopped black olives	125 mL
½ cup	chopped red onion	125 mL
½ cup	chopped red pepper	125 mL
½ cup	chopped green pepper	125 mL
1 cup	grated mozzarella cheese	250 mL

Crust: Preheat oven to 425°F (220°C). In a large bowl, combine flour, cornmeal, chili powder, cumin and salt. With a pastry blender or 2 knives, cut in butter until fine crumbs form. With a fork, stir in water just until mixture clings together. Form into a ball. Roll out pastry to fit a 9 x 13" (23 x 33 cm) flan pan or baking dish. Prick pastry bottom with a fork. Bake for 25-35 minutes, or until golden brown around edges. Remove from oven and set aside to cool.

Zesty Bean Appetizer Flan Continued

Filling: Purée or mash beans. Add salsa, green onions, garlic, sour cream, lemon juice, salt and pepper; mix well. Spread filling in cooled pastry shell.

Topping: In a large bowl, combine olives, onion, peppers and cheese; sprinkle over the filling. Refrigerate until ready to serve. Cut into squares.

Makes 24 squares Serves 10-12

Variation: For a quick and easy version, omit the crust and spread the filling evenly in a shallow bowl or pie plate. Add toppings and refrigerate. Spread on crackers to serve.

Pictured on the back cover.

Mexican Party Spread

Here is an easy layered spread for around the campfire or barbecue.

8 oz.	cream cheese, softened	250 g
½ cup	mayonnaise	125 mL
⅔ cup	salsa	150 mL
1 cup	chopped cooked ham	250 mL
¾ cup	shredded Cheddar cheese	175 mL
¾ cup	shredded mozzarella cheese	175 mL
½ cup	chopped green pepper	125 mL
¼ cup	sliced black olives	60 mL

In a small bowl, combine cream cheese and mayonnaise; beat together until smooth. Spread evenly over a 12" (30 cm) round plate or serving platter. Spread salsa on top, leaving a small border around the edge. Sprinkle ham, cheeses, green pepper and olives on top. Cover and chill until ready to serve. Serve with corn chips.

Serves 6-8

Pictured on the back cover.

Baked Double Cheese Dip

Layered baked dip. Great as an appetizer or as a snack while sitting around the campfire.

8 oz.	cream cheese, softened	250 g
½ tsp.	dried oregano	2 mL
½ tsp.	dried basil	2 mL
2	garlic cloves, minced	2
4-6 drops	hot pepper sauce	4-6 drops
2 cups	shredded mozzarella cheese	500 mL
1 cup	shredded Cheddar cheese	250 mL
½ cup	tomato sauce	125 mL
½ cup	finely chopped green pepper	125 mL
½ cup	finely chopped red pepper	125 mL

Preheat oven to 350°F (180°C). In a small bowl, combine cream cheese, oregano, basil, garlic and hot pepper sauce; mix well. Spread cheese mixture evenly in a lightly buttered 9" pie plate. Combine mozzarella and Cheddar cheeses and sprinkle half over the cream cheese layer. Top with the tomato sauce and peppers. Sprinkle with the remaining cheese. Bake for 20-25 minutes. Serve warm with toasted pitas, tortilla chips or breadsticks.

Makes 3½ cups (875 mL)

Note: For outdoor cooking, this dip may be combined in a heatproof grilling dish. Preheat grill for 10 minutes. Set the dish over indirect, medium heat and cook for 30-35 minutes.

🌲 To make area rugs for your RV or tent, use bath mats – they shake clean easily and are soft underfoot.

Salads & Side Dishes

Fresh Fruit
Fruit & Greens
Vegetables

Champagne Fruit Salad

The perfect choice for a Champagne Picnic or any special occasion. Use any combination of seasonal fruits. Combine the fruit and sugar syrup up to 12 hours before serving and refrigerate. Add champagne just before serving.

1	orange, peeled and sectioned	1
1	apple, cored and chopped	1
1	kiwi fruit, sliced	1
1 cup	chopped cantaloupe	250 mL
1 cup	green grapes	250 mL
1 cup	halved strawberries	250 mL
1 tbsp.	lemon juice	15 mL
¾ cup	water	175 mL
¼ cup	sugar	60 mL
1½ cups	dry champagne	375 mL

Peel and chop fruit into chunks or pieces of uniform size. In a small saucepan, combine lemon juice, water and sugar; stir to combine. Place over medium heat and bring to a boil, remove from heat and cool to room temperature; pour over fruit and refrigerate until serving. Top with chilled champagne just before serving.

Serves 8-10

Summer Fruit Salad/Pineapple Lime Dressing

Using the fruits of the summer season, start your day with this great salad.

2	peaches, peeled, pitted, sliced	2
2	oranges, peeled, sectioned	2
2 cups	hulled, sliced strawberries	500 mL
1 cup	green grapes	250 mL
1 cup	melon balls	250 mL

Summer Fruit Salad Continued

Pineapple Lime Dressing:

½ cup	pineapple juice	125 mL
½ tsp.	grated lime peel	2 mL
¼ tsp.	ground ginger OR 1 tsp. (5 mL) grated fresh	1 mL
3 tbsp.	EACH lime juice and honey	45 mL

In a large bowl, combine all fruit. To make dressing, in a small bowl, combine all dressing ingredients. Whisk until blended. Pour over fruit and stir gently to coat. Serve immediately.

Serves 4-6

Fresh Fruit and Berry Salad

This salad is a colorful addition to any breakfast or brunch table.

1	fresh pineapple, peeled, cored, cubed	1
3	apples, cored, cubed	3
1	small cantaloupe, cubed	1
1	large banana, sliced	1
2 cups	EACH halved strawberries, blueberries, seedless red or green grapes	500 mL
3	kiwi fruit, peeled, sliced	3

Creamy Lemon Dressing:

3 oz.	cream cheese, softened	85 g
½ cup	icing (confectioner's) sugar	125 mL
2 tsp.	lemon juice	10 mL
8 oz.	frozen whipped topping, thawed	250 g

In a 4-quart (4 L) glass serving bowl, combine all fruits and berries, toss to combine. In a mixing bowl, with an electric mixer, beat cream cheese until smooth. Gradually add sugar and lemon juice; mix well. Fold in whipped topping. Spread over fruit. Serve immediately.

Serves 12-15

Variation: Serve the salad with a dollop of the dressing on the side.

Mediterranean Bread Salad

The bread cubes in this salad are like fresh croûtons. They absorb the garlicky dressing and are very flavorful. A Lebanese version uses lightly toasted pita.

2 tbsp.	vegetable oil	30 mL
1	medium onion, sliced	1
2	medium zucchini, cut into ½" (1.3 cm) slices	2
½ lb.	fresh mushrooms, sliced	250 g
1	red pepper, seeded, cut into strips	1
3-4 cups	fresh Italian bread, cut into 1" (2.5 cm) cubes	750 mL-1 L
2 cups	EACH torn romaine and leaf lettuce	500 mL
¼ lb.	pepperoni, thinly sliced	125 mL

Basil Vinaigrette:

½ cup	olive oil	125 mL
¼ cup	red wine vinegar	60 mL
2 tsp.	dried basil	10 mL
3	garlic cloves, minced	3
½ tsp.	salt	2 mL
¼ tsp.	pepper	1 mL

In a frying pan over medium heat, heat oil. Add onion and sauté until just soft, 1-2 minutes. Add zucchini and cook just until tender, approximately 4-5 minutes. Transfer onion and zucchini to a large bowl. Add mushrooms and red pepper to frying pan; sauté just until wilted, 1-2 minutes. Add them to the zucchini mixture. Cover vegetables and refrigerate until cold.

To prepare the vinaigrette, in a jar with a tight -fitting lid, combine all vinaigrette ingredients. Shake well and set aside.

Just before serving, place the bread cubes in a salad bowl. Shake the vinaigrette; sprinkle half over the bread cubes. Add cooked vegetables; toss well with bread cubes. Add lettuce, pepperoni and remaining vinaigrette; toss well and serve.

Serves 8-10

Pictured on page 103.

Broccoli, Sprout and Snow Pea Salad

Tangy and refreshing, this salad is great for a summer brunch.

1 tbsp.	sesame seeds, toasted	15 mL
½ lb.	snow peas	250 g
½ lb.	broccoli	250 g
2 cups	bean sprouts	500 mL
2	green onions, chopped	2

Lemon and Oil Dressing:

¼ cup	lemon juice	60 mL
¼ cup	vegetable oil	60 mL
2 tsp.	sugar	10 mL
½ tsp.	ground ginger	2 mL
4-6 drops	hot pepper sauce	4-6 drops

Place the sesame seeds in a small frying pan over medium heat. Stirring constantly, cook until golden brown, 2-3 minutes. Immediately remove from heat and transfer to a paper towel to cool completely. Cut tops and tails from snow peas and place in a large bowl, break broccoli into florets and add to snow peas. Add bean sprouts and green onions; toss lightly to combine. In a small jar with a tight-fitting lid, combine all dressing ingredients; shake well. Pour over vegetables; toss to coat. Sprinkle with sesame seeds and serve immediately.

Serves 4-6

For camping or back packing, take individual packets of mayonnaise, soy sauce, ketchup, relish, mustard, hot sauce, Parmesan cheese, hot peppers, etc., instead of taking larger containers of each. These can be purchased at wholesale/discount stores.

Sprouts with Vegetable Julienne

Colorful and easy-for the sprout lover, this is Jacquie's specialty.

2	red peppers, seeded, cut julienne	2
2	green peppers, seeded, cut julienne	2
3	celery sticks, cut into thin strips	3
2	carrots, peeled and cut into thin strips	2
1 cup	alfalfa sprouts	250 mL

Mustard Dressing:

½ cup	French salad dressing	125 mL
1 tbsp.	prepared mustard	15 mL

In a large bowl, combine all cut vegetables, add alfalfa sprouts and toss lightly to combine. In a small bowl, gradually stir French dressing into the mustard. Mix well and pour over vegetables; toss lightly to coat. Serve immediately.

Serves 4-6

Cauliflower and Broccoli Salad with Green Grapes

This highly portable salad is served by Jo's ladies' group at the Everdell hall near Rocky Mountain House. It is a hit with all their guests.

3 cups	cauliflower, cut into bite-sized florets	750 mL
3 cups	broccoli, cut into bite-sized florets	750 mL
1	small red onion, sliced, separated	1
1	green OR red pepper, seeded, chopped	1
1 cup	sliced celery	250 mL
1½ cups	green grapes, halved	375 mL

Sour Cream Dressing:

1 cup	sour cream	250 mL
¾ cup	mayonnaise	175 mL
½ tsp.	salt	2 mL
¼ tsp.	pepper	1 mL

Cauliflower and Broccoli Salad Continued

In a large salad bowl, combine cauliflower, broccoli, onion, pepper, celery and grapes; toss to combine. In a small bowl, mix together sour cream and mayonnaise; add salt and pepper to taste. Mix well and pour over salad in bowl. Toss well and serve immediately.

Serves 10-12

Pictured on page 121.

Pictured on page 121.

Apple Pecan Salad with Creamy Spiced Dressing

Colorful, spicy and delicious. Serve with pork or ham dishes.

2	**Granny Smith apples**	2
2	**Red Delicious apples**	2
2 tbsp.	lemon juice	30 mL
1½ cups	thinly sliced celery	375 mL
½ cup	pecan halves, toasted	125 mL

Creamy Spiced Dressing:

½ cup	mayonnaise	125 mL
½ cup	sour cream	125 mL
2 tsp.	lemon juice	10 mL
1 tsp.	liquid honey	5 mL
⅛ tsp.	ground cinnamon	0.5 mL
⅛ tsp.	ground nutmeg	0.5 mL

Core and thinly slice all apples; dip slices in lemon juice so they do not discolor. Place in a large bowl. Add celery and pecans; toss lightly. In a small bowl, combine all dressing ingredients, mix well and pour over apple mixture. Toss lightly to coat. Serve immediately.

Serves 4-6

German Cucumber Salad

This cool, light salad has an exhilarating fresh flavor.

2	medium cucumbers, thinly sliced	2
4	green onions, thinly sliced	4
3	small tomatoes, sliced	3
2 tbsp.	snipped fresh parsley	30 mL

Creamy Dill Dressing:

¼ cup	sour cream	60 mL
¼ tsp.	prepared mustard	1 mL
2 tbsp.	minced fresh dill	30 mL
1 tbsp.	EACH vinegar and milk	15 mL
½ tsp.	salt	2 mL
⅛ tsp.	pepper	0.5 mL

In a large salad bowl, combine cucumbers, onions, tomatoes and parsley. In a small bowl, combine all dressing ingredients. Pour over cucumber mixture and toss gently. Cover and chill for at least 1 hour.

Serves 4-6

Mediterranean Red Onion Salad

2	large red onions, very thinly sliced	2
1 cup	halved black Greek olives	250 mL
¼ cup	vegetable oil	60 mL
1 tbsp.	soy sauce	15 mL
1½ tsp.	dry white wine	7 mL
1½ tsp.	red wine vinegar	7 mL
¼ tsp.	pepper	1 mL
1 tbsp.	finely chopped fresh parsley	15 mL
¼ cup	freshly grated Parmesan cheese	60 mL

Separate onions into rings. Arrange onions and olives in shallow salad bowl. In a small bowl, combine oil, soy sauce, wine, vinegar and pepper. Pour over onions. Cover and refrigerate for 4 hours. Just before serving, toss salad and sprinkle with parsley and Parmesan.

Serves 4

Pictured on page 85.

Asparagus Vinaigrette

Dijon Vinaigrette:

1½ cups	olive oil OR vegetable oil	375 mL
½ cup	wine vinegar	125 mL
2 tsp.	Dijon mustard	10 mL
½ tsp.	salt	2 mL
⅛ tsp.	pepper	0.5 mL
4	large radishes, sliced	4
¼ cup	chopped green pepper	60 mL
¼ cup	finely chopped dill pickles	60 mL
1 tsp.	dried parsley flakes	5 mL
2	green onions, finely chopped	2
2 lbs.	fresh asparagus spears, cooked tender-crisp, drained	1 kg
3	hard-boiled eggs, shelled, sliced	3
2	medium tomatoes, cut into wedges lettuce leaves	2

In a large bowl, whisk together the oil, vinegar, mustard, salt and pepper. Add radishes, green pepper, dill pickles, parsley and green onions. Place cooked asparagus in a single layer in a glass dish; pour dressing over top. Cover and chill at least 4 hours or overnight.

To serve: Arrange lettuce on a serving platter; remove asparagus and vegetables from dressing with a slotted spoon and arrange over lettuce. Garnish with egg slices and tomato wedges. Drizzle with 3-4 tbsp. (45-60 mL) of the dressing. Remaining dressing may be served on the side if additional dressing is desired.

Serves 6-8

Kidney Bean Salad with Chili Dressing

2 tsp.	chili powder	10 mL
¼ cup	vegetable oil	60 mL
2 tbsp.	vinegar	30 mL
2 tsp.	sugar	10 mL
¼ tsp.	salt	1 mL
2 x 19 oz.	cans kidney beans, drained	2 x 540 mL
1 cup	diced green pepper	250 mL
1	chopped red onion	1
1 cup	halved pitted black olives	250 mL
2 tbsp.	ketchup	30 mL
1 tbsp.	mayonnaise	15 mL
1 head	iceberg lettuce	1 head
1 cup	shredded Cheddar cheese	250 mL

In a small saucepan over medium heat, combine chili powder and vegetable oil. Heat for 2-3 minutes to develop flavor. Remove from heat; stir in vinegar, sugar and salt; set aside. Drain kidney beans and place in a large bowl. Pour over the heated chili vegetable oil mixture. Stir to combine and let stand approximately 30 minutes to season. Stir in green pepper, onion, olives, ketchup and mayonnaise; toss lightly to mix. The salad my be prepared to this point, covered and refrigerated for up to 24 hours. When ready to serve, shred lettuce coarsely and place in a large salad bowl. Spoon bean mixture over lettuce. Sprinkle shredded cheese on top. Serve immediately with additional shredded cheese and sour cream.

Serves 6-8

Tomato and Mozzarella Salad

Quick and easy. Just add a loaf of Italian bread and lunch is ready.

4	tomatoes, sliced	4
1	small Spanish onion, sliced thinly	1
8	slices mozzarella cheese	8
¾ cup	Italian salad dressing	175 mL

In a medium bowl, layer tomatoes, onion and cheese. Pour Italian dressing over salad. Cover and marinate 2-4 hours. Garnish with fresh parsley.

Serves 4

Picnic Coleslaw

This recipe has an oil and vinegar dressing which is great for make ahead or storing. If you prefer a creamy dressing, use our Creamy Dill Dressing variation.

3 cups	shredded cabbage	750 mL
1 cup	shredded carrots	250 mL
5 strips	bacon, cooked crisp and crumbled	5 strips
½ cup	green onions, thinly sliced	125 mL

Cider Vinegar and Oil Dressing:

½ cup	cider vinegar	125 mL
⅓ cup	vegetable oil	75 mL
⅓ cup	sugar	75 mL
1 tsp.	salt	5 mL

In a large bowl, combine cabbage, carrots, bacon and onions. In a small jar, with a tight-fitting lid, combine vinegar, oil, sugar and salt; shake well. Just before serving, pour dressing over cabbage mixture and toss.

Serves 6-8

Variation: Creamy Dill Dressing: 1 cup (250 mL) mayonnaise, ⅓ cup (75 mL) finely chopped dill pickles and 3-4 tbsp. (45-60 mL) dill pickle juice. Stir well and pour over salad.

Marinated Mushroom Salad

A tasty make-ahead, bring-along salad, this is great for potlucks and picnics.

8-10 cups	water	2-2.5 L
3 tbsp.	lemon juice	45 mL
3 lbs.	small fresh mushrooms, cleaned	1.5 kg
2	carrots, sliced	2
1 cup	sliced celery	250 mL
1 cup	chopped green pepper	250 mL
½ cup	chopped red onion	125 mL
1 tsp.	dried parsley flakes	5 mL
½ cup	sliced stuffed olives	125 mL
1 cup	sliced black Greek olives	250 mL

Garlic and Red Wine Italian Dressing:

½ cup	Italian salad dressing	125 mL
½ cup	red wine vinegar	125 mL
2	garlic cloves, minced	2
½ tsp.	dried oregano	2 mL
½ tsp.	salt	2 mL

In a large saucepan, combine water and lemon juice; set over medium-high heat and bring to a boil. Add mushrooms and cook for 3 minutes, stirring occasionally. Drain and cool. Place cooled mushrooms in a large bowl; add carrots, celery, green pepper, onion, parsley and olives. Stir to combine. In a small jar with a tight-fitting lid, combine Italian dressing, vinegar, garlic, oregano and salt; shake well. Pour over salad. Cover and refrigerate overnight.

Serves 6-8

Greek Lemon, Herb Potato Salad

A different twist for potato salad, this is nice and light with the herbed lemon dressing.

25-30	new baby potatoes, washed and halved	25-30
1	red pepper, seeded, chopped	1
1	green pepper, seeded, chopped	1
4	small tomatoes, quartered	4
1	small red onion, sliced	1
⅔ cup	sliced black Greek olives	150 mL
½ cup	cubed feta cheese	125 mL

Herbed Lemon Dressing:

⅓ cup	olive oil	75 mL
1 tbsp.	lemon juice	15 mL
3	garlic cloves, minced	3
1 tsp.	dried dillweed	5 mL
2 tsp.	dried thyme	10 mL

Boil, steam or microwave potatoes until tender; cool. In a large bowl, combine potatoes, peppers, tomatoes, onion, olives and feta cheese. Mix gently to combine.

Dressing: In a small jar with a tight-fitting lid, combine all dressing ingredients. Shake well and pour over potato mixture; toss gently. This salad may be prepared a day ahead and stored, covered, in the refrigerator.

Serves 6-8

Pictured on page 85.

Potato Salad

Is it possible to have a picnic without everyone's favorite – the potato salad? Here you have several excellent choices: three sisters – three versions!

2 lbs.	small red potatoes, with skins	1 kg

Sour Cream-Mustard Dressing:

1 cup	sour cream	250 mL
2 tbsp.	Dijon mustard	30 mL
2 tbsp.	chopped fresh dill	30 mL
¼ tsp.	EACH salt and pepper	1 mL

Parsley-Green Onion Dressing:

1 cup	mayonnaise	250 mL
½ cup	chopped green onions	125 mL
½ cup	chopped celery	125 mL
¼ cup	chopped fresh parsley	60 mL
½ tsp.	EACH salt and pepper	2 mL

Classic Dressing:

1 cup	mayonnaise	250 mL
2	hard-cooked eggs, peeled, chopped	2
2	large dill pickles, finely chopped	2
½ cup	chopped green onion	125 mL
½ tsp.	EACH salt and pepper	2 mL
	crumbled crisp bacon	

Scrub potatoes, leaving skins on. Place potatoes in saucepan and bring to a boil over high heat. Reduce heat to medium; cook until tender, about 20 minutes. Drain and cool. Cut potatoes into 1" (2.5 cm) cubes.

Sour Cream-Mustard Dressing: In a large bowl, combine sour cream and mustard; add dill, salt and pepper; mix well. Add potatoes to dressing in bowl; toss gently to coat potatoes evenly. Cover and refrigerate for 2-4 hours. Before serving, garnish with fresh dill sprigs if desired.

Parsley-Green Onion Dressing: In a large bowl, combine all dressing ingredients. Add potatoes and mix as above. Garnish with parsley sprigs.

Classic Dressing: In a large bowl, combine mayonnaise, eggs, pickles, onion, salt and pepper. Gently stir in potatoes. Garnish with bacon.

Serves 4-6

Fisherman's Lunch

Baked Potato Salad

Baking the potatoes gives them a different texture and flavor.

2 lbs.	potatoes, peeled and cut into ¾" (2 cm) cubes	1 kg
2 tbsp.	vegetable oil	30 mL
1 oz.	pkg. Ranch OR Italian salad dressing mix	30 g
1	green pepper, seeded, chopped	1
3	green onions, chopped	3
1	large tomato, chopped	1
3	hard-cooked eggs, peeled, chopped	3
½ cup	celery, chopped	125 mL
5 strips	bacon, cooked crisp, crumbled	5 strips

Creamy Basil Garlic Dressing:

¾ cup	mayonnaise	175 mL
1 tbsp.	vinegar	15 mL
2 tsp.	lemon juice	10 mL
1 tsp.	dried basil	5 mL
½ tsp.	salt	2 mL
¼ tsp.	pepper	1 mL
1	garlic clove, minced	1

Preheat oven to 400°F (200°C). In a large bowl, toss the potatoes with the oil and the salad dressing mix. Place potatoes in a lightly buttered 9 x 13" (23 x 33 cm) baking pan. Bake, uncovered, for 45 minutes, or until tender. Remove from oven and cool. Transfer potatoes to a large salad bowl and add pepper, onion, tomato, eggs, celery and bacon. Toss gently. In a small bowl, combine all dressing ingredients; mix well. Pour over salad and stir gently. Cover and refrigerate for at least 1 hour for flavors to combine.

Serves 8-10

Variation: The potatoes could be baked in foil on a grill if you are camping, and can plan ahead for your next meal.

Seafood Pasta Salad

½ cup	mayonnaise	125 mL
¼ cup	Italian salad dressing	60 mL
2 tbsp.	grated Parmesan cheese	30 mL
19 oz.	can chickpeas, drained and rinsed	540 mL
2-3 cups	cooked corkscrew pasta, rinsed, drained	500-750 mL
8 oz.	chopped imitation crab meat (pollock)*	250 g
1 cup	broccoli florets	250 mL
½ cup	chopped green peppers	125 mL
½ cup	chopped tomato	125 mL
¼ cup	sliced green onion	60 mL

In a large bowl, combine mayonnaise, Italian dressing and cheese; stir to blend well. Add chickpeas, pasta, crab meat, broccoli, green peppers, tomato and onion; toss gently to mix. Cover and refrigerate for at least 2 hours for flavors to blend.

Serves 4-6

* Or the real thing if you're camping near the ocean or it's a celebration.

Strawberry, Orange and Beef Salad

This hearty salad is a meal in itself, the fresh fruit is a wonderful flavor combination with the cold beef.

1 lb.	cold cooked steak or roast beef	500 g
1 bunch	fresh spinach	1 bunch
2	oranges, peeled, sectioned	2
2 cups	cleaned, halved fresh strawberries	500 mL
	ranch salad dressing	

Slice leftover beef into thin slices; place in a bowl and set aside. Wash spinach; drain and set aside. Add oranges and strawberries to beef; toss lightly. Tear spinach and arrange in the bottom of a salad bowl; add beef and fruit mixture. Add ranch salad dressing and toss gently to combine. Serve immediately with fresh rolls or bread.

Serves 4

Pictured on page 35.

Green Grape and Mandarin Chicken Supreme Salad

This great brunch or lunch salad uses leftover chicken or turkey.

1 cup	mayonnaise	250 mL
¼ cup	lime juice	60 mL
1 tsp.	salt	5 mL
¼ tsp.	nutmeg	1 mL
4 cups	cooked chicken or turkey, cubed	1 L
10 oz.	can mandarin orange segments, drained	284 mL
1 cup	halved seedless green grapes	250 mL
¾ cup	chopped celery	175 mL
½ cup	toasted slivered almonds lettuce for garnish	125 mL

In a large bowl, combine mayonnaise, lime juice, salt and nutmeg. Add all remaining ingredients, except lettuce; mix well. Cover and chill in refrigerator for 2 hours. Serve on a bed of lettuce.

Serves 4-6

Grilled Mushrooms

A must side dish with steak.

1 lb.	whole fresh mushrooms, cleaned	500 g
½ cup	butter OR margarine, melted	125 mL
1 tsp.	dried dillweed	5 mL
1 tsp.	garlic salt	5 mL

Thread mushrooms on 10-12" skewers. In a small bowl, combine butter, dillweed and garlic salt. Brush over mushrooms. Grill over hot coals for 10-15 minutes, basting and turning every 5 minutes. Serve immediately.

Serves 6-8

Grilled Italian Vegetables

Cooked in foil packets, the Italian dressing adds a tantalizing flavor to these vegetables.

4	potatoes, thinly sliced	4
1	onion, thinly sliced	1
4	carrots, thinly sliced	4
1	zucchini, sliced	1
2	green peppers, seeded, sliced	2
¼ cup	Italian salad dressing	60 mL
½ tsp.	salt	2 mL
½ tsp.	Italian seasoning	2 mL
¼ tsp.	pepper	1 mL
2	ice cubes	2
	sour cream	

Preheat grill for 10 minutes to medium heat. Divide potatoes, onions, carrots, zucchini and peppers in half and arrange on double thicknesses of heavy-duty aluminum foil to make 2 packets. Divide Italian salad dressing, salt, Italian seasoning and pepper and sprinkle on each portion. Add 1 ice cube to each packet. Wrap foil into square shapes; fold edges under and press to seal. Bake over direct medium heat; turning packets over 3-4 times until vegetables are tender, 20-25 minutes. Serve immediately with sour cream.

Serves 4-6

Variation: For ***Fast, Fast, Herbed Grilled Vegetables***, julienne carrots and zucchini (they'll cook faster), add sliced mushrooms. Arrange on foil as above, but make 4 packets. Drizzle with equal amounts of butter and lemon juice, sprinkle with garlic salt, dried basil and thyme. Fold foil into packets as above and grill for 10 minutes.

Grilled Corn

Fresh corn on the cob is one of the supreme treats of summer. Here are two options for grilling.

In Husks: Gently peel husks back to within 2" (5 cm) of the base. Remove silk and smooth husks back into place, completely covering the kernels. Using kitchen twine, tie husks in several places to secure. Fill a sink or a large saucepan with ice water and soak corn for 30 minutes to 1 hour. Drain and shake off excess water.

Preheat the grill. Generously oil the grill to prevent sticking. Grill corn directly over medium to medium-hot coals, 5" (13 cm) from the heat, turning occasionally until tender, approximately 30-45 minutes, or until husks are dry and browned. Remove string and husks and serve corn immediately with butter, flavored butter or margarine, see page 135.

Variation: For **Bacon Ears**, turn back husks; remove the silk. Wrap a strip of bacon around each ear of corn; toothpick in place if necessary. Replace the husks and prepare as above. When corn is almost done, remove husk and grill corn directly to crisp bacon.

Variation: For **Herbed Grilled Corn**, after corn is soaked and drained as above, spread a mixture of herbed butter, see page 135, or try a mixture of basil, marjoram, salt, pepper, paprika, onion flakes, generously over each cob. Rewrap husks, then wrap each ear of corn in foil. Grill as above for 25 minutes.

Foil Wrapped: Husk corn and remove all silk particles. Tear off 4 paper towels. Cut 4 pieces of heavy-duty aluminum foil, each slightly larger than the paper towels. Place 1 paper towel on each piece of foil. Pour ¼ cup (60 mL) of water onto each square. Place corn on wet paper towel and roll up. Fold foil ends under and press edges to seal. Preheat the grill. Grill directly over medium coals 5-6" (13-15 cm) from heat; turn cobs 3-4 times until tender, approximately 25-35 minutes. Remove foil wrap and serve immediately with butter, flavored butters or margarine, see page 135.

Serves 4

Pictured on the front cover.

Grilled Cheesy Vegetable Zucchini Boats

Any vegetables can be used in this recipe, it's a very showy, delicious dish.

6	medium zucchini	6
1 tbsp.	butter OR margarine	15 mL
1	onion, finely chopped	1
1	garlic clove, minced	1
1 tbsp.	flour	15 mL
½ cup	milk	125 mL
¼ tsp.	salt	1 mL
⅛ tsp.	pepper	0.5 mL
1 cup	grated Cheddar cheese	250 mL
4 cups	cooked mixed vegetables	1 L
1 tsp.	dried dillweed	5 mL
10-12	slices bacon, cooked crisp, crumbled	10-12
2 tbsp.	grated Parmesan cheese	30 mL

Place zucchini in a large pan of boiling water; boil for 3 minutes; drain. Split zucchini in half lengthwise; scoop out pulp. Set aside. In a frying pan, over medium heat, melt butter; add onion and garlic and cook until tender, 2-3 minutes. Add flour; cook for 1 minute, stirring constantly. Gradually stir in milk; cook and stir until sauce boils and thickens. Add salt, pepper and cheese; stir until melted. Add cooked vegetables and dillweed; stir to combine. Fill zucchini with vegetable mixture; place in a heatproof 10 x 15" (25 x 38 cm) baking pan. Sprinkle with crumbled bacon and Parmesan cheese. Cover loosely with foil. Grill until filling is hot, 15-25 minutes.

Serves 6

Pictured on page 155.

Cheesy Spinach Bake

To bake or grill, this is a great side dish or brunch dish.

2 x 10 oz.	frozen chopped spinach	2 x 284 g
2 cups	cooked rice	500 mL
2 cups	shredded Cheddar cheese	500 mL
4	eggs, beaten	4
⅔ cup	milk	150 mL
¼ cup	butter OR margarine, softened	60 mL
¼ cup	chopped onion	60 mL
2 tsp.	salt	10 mL
2 tsp.	Worcestershire sauce	10 mL

Preheat oven to 350°F (180°C). Cook spinach according to package directions; drain well, squeezing out excess liquid. In a large bowl, combine spinach, rice, cheese, eggs, milk, butter, onion, salt and Worcestershire sauce. Stir well. Pour spinach mixture into a lightly buttered 9 x 13" (23 x 33 cm) baking dish. Cover and bake for 20 minutes. Uncover and bake for an additional 5-10 minutes, or until set.

Serves 12-15

To grill: Preheat grill for 10 minutes. Place spinach mixture in a heat-proof grilling pan; cover with foil and place over medium indirect heat. Cook as above for 25-30 minutes. Uncover and cook for an additional 10 minutes.

🌲 **If there is nothing else available, empty tin cans make great (if small) cooking pots. Before using, tins should be held over a fire to remove the lacquer lining and then washed in scalding water with a strong detergent.**

Zesty Carrot Bake

A creamy, tangy side dish, this can accompany any barbecued meat or fish.

1 lb.	fresh carrots, cut into ½" (1.3 cm) slices	500 g
2 tbsp.	minced onion	30 mL
¾ cup	mayonnaise	175 mL
⅓ cup	water	75 mL
1 tbsp.	prepared horseradish	15 mL
¼ tsp.	pepper	1 mL
½ cup	dry bread crumbs	125 mL
2 tbsp.	butter OR margarine, melted	30 mL
½ cup	shredded Cheddar cheese	125 mL

Preheat oven to 350°F (180°C). Cook carrots in boiling water until tender crisp. Drain and place in a 1-quart (1 L) baking dish; set aside. In a small bowl, combine onion, mayonnaise, water, horseradish and pepper; mix well and pour over carrots. Combine the bread crumbs with the melted butter; sprinkle over carrots. Bake, uncovered, for 25-30 minutes. Remove carrots from oven and sprinkle with the cheese. Return to oven and bake for an additional 3-5 minutes, or until cheese is melted. Serve immediately.

Serves 6

Note: Or pour carrot mixture into a heatproof grilling pan and cover with foil. Preheat grill for 10 minutes. Grill over indirect medium heat for 30-40 minutes. Serve as above.

To grill carrots, potatoes or sweet potatoes directly on a grill, slice them in thick slices, brush with vegetable oil and pierce them with a fork. Grill over medium heat until tender.

Parmesan Green Bean Stir-Fry

Pick up fresh green beans at the Farmer's Market and cook this on the grill.

1 lb.	fresh or frozen whole green beans	500 g
6 tbsp.	butter OR margarine	90 mL
3	garlic cloves, minced	3
¼ cup	chopped onion	60 mL
2 cups	sliced mushrooms	500 mL
¼ cup	grated Parmesan cheese	60 mL

Cook green beans in water until tender crisp. Drain and set aside. In a large frying pan, over medium-low heat, melt butter and sauté garlic and onions for 1 minute; add mushrooms and cook until tender. Add green beans and toss well until beans are heated through. Pour into a serving dish and sprinkle with Parmesan cheese.

Serves 6

Parmesan Potatoes in Foil

3	large baking potatoes, sliced	3
1	onion, sliced	1
¼ tsp.	celery salt	1 mL
¼ tsp.	pepper	1 mL
½ cup	grated Parmesan cheese	125 mL
¼ cup	butter or margarine	60 mL

Scrub potatoes, do not peel; slice into ¼" (1 cm) slices. Spread potatoes on a 20" (50 cm) length of foil. Scatter sliced onions over top; sprinkle with celery salt and pepper. Top with grated cheese and dot with butter. Bring edges of foil together and fold. Double wrap with a second sheet of foil. Place wrapped potatoes on a grill over direct heat and grill for 30-45 minutes, or until cooked, turning several times. Serve immediately.

Serves 4

Campfire Potatoes

Cook potatoes and onions in a zippy cheese sauce in foil packages.

5	medium potatoes, peeled, thinly sliced	5
1	onion, sliced	1
½ cup	butter OR margarine	125 mL
½ cup	shredded Cheddar cheese	125 mL
1 tbsp.	dried parsley	15 mL
1 tbsp.	Worcestershire sauce	15 mL
⅛ tsp.	pepper	0.5 mL
⅓ cup	chicken OR beef broth	75 mL

Place the potatoes and onion on a large piece of heavy-duty foil; dot with butter. In a small bowl, combine the cheese, parsley, Worcestershire sauce and pepper; stir well; sprinkle over potatoes. Fold foil up around potatoes and add broth. Seal the edges of the foil well; wrap foil packet in a second sheet of foil; wrapping edges well. Grill over medium coals for 35-45 minutes, or until potatoes are tender. Serve immediately.

Serves 4-6

 A tin-can stove can be easily made by taking an ordinary large can and cutting one hole in the lower part of one side for fuel and another hole near the top for a crossdraft. It requires very little fuel; a few twigs or a couple of candles is all that is necessary to cook a hot snack.

Cheddar Au Gratin Potatoes

These creamy, cheesy potatoes are made with hash browns. They are wonderful with grilled ham or steak, or as a brunch dish.

¼ cup	flour	60 mL
½ tsp.	salt	2 mL
⅛ tsp.	pepper	0.5 mL
2 x 12 oz.	frozen shredded hash brown potatoes, thawed	2 x 340 mL
¼ cup	chopped onion	60 mL
1 cup	shredded Cheddar cheese	250 mL
1½ cups	half-and-half cereal cream	375 mL

Preheat grill for 10 minutes to medium heat. In a large plastic food storage bag, combine flour, salt and pepper. Add potatoes; shake to coat. Lightly butter a 1½-quart (1.5 L) grill-safe casserole. Place half of the potato mixture in the casserole. Sprinkle with half of the onion and half of the cheese. Layer with remaining potato mixture, onion and cheese. Pour cream over layers. Cover with foil. Using indirect medium heat, bake until potatoes are tender and sauce thickens, approximately 1-1½ hours.

Serves 4-6

❋ Buy fresh vegetables and fruit at a farmers' market or roadside stands. For best flavor use the fruits and vegetables that are in season. You can grill them over direct heat or place them in foil packets and cook on the grill.

Apple and Bacon Baked Beans

The flavors mingle during the long baking period to produce this irresistible Canadian speciality.

4 cups	dried white beans	1 L
19 oz.	can tomatoes with liquid, crushed	540 mL
1 cup	maple syrup	250 mL
2 tsp.	cider vinegar	10 mL
1 tbsp.	dry mustard	15 mL
2 tsp.	salt	10 mL
¼ tsp.	ground ginger	1 mL
2	apples, peeled, cored, chopped	2
½ lb.	bacon, cut into bite-sized pieces	250 g
1	large onion, sliced	1

Sort and wash beans, discarding blemished ones. Place in a large saucepan; add enough water to cover beans by about 2" (5 cm). Set beans over medium-high heat and bring to a boil; cover and cook for 2 minutes. Remove from heat and let stand, covered, for 1 hour.

Pour in enough additional water to cover beans by about 2" (5 cm). Set over heat again and bring to a boil. Reduce heat and simmer for 45 minutes, or until beans are slightly soft. Drain.

Preheat oven to 250°F (120°C). Transfer beans to a bean pot or Dutch oven with a lid. Stir in tomatoes, maple syrup, vinegar, mustard, salt and ginger. Add chopped apples, bacon pieces and sliced onion; stir to combine. Add just enough boiling water to cover the beans. Cover and bake for 5-6 hours, adding boiling water occasionally to maintain liquid level. Stir beans occasionally from bottom of pot to top so they cook evenly. Remove the lid during the last hour of cooking.

Serves 10-12

One-Dish Dinners

Tacos

Fajitas

Casseroles

Stews

Chili

Scallop Mushroom Tacos

A mild dill-flavored taco for seafood lovers, you can add more zest* if that is your preference. Scallops cook very quickly – don't overcook or they will be tough.

2 tbsp.	butter OR margarine	30 mL
½ lb.	fresh scallops, thinly sliced	250 g
1 lb.	fresh mushrooms, sliced	500 g
½ cup	chopped celery	125 mL
2 tbsp.	finely chopped onion	30 mL
¼ tsp.	salt	1 mL
⅛ tsp.	pepper	0.5 mL
½ cup	dry white wine	125 mL
1 cup	chicken stock	250 mL
1 tbsp.	cornstarch	15 mL
2 tbsp.	cold water	30 mL
1 tsp.	dillweed	5 mL
1½ cups	cooked rice	375 mL
	shredded lettuce; grated Cheddar cheese, chopped tomatoes	
4	taco shells, warmed	4

Heat butter in a large frying pan over medium heat. As soon as the pan is hot, add the scallops, mushrooms, celery and onion. Season with salt and pepper and cook for 2-3 minutes. Add wine and hot chicken stock; bring to a boil. Reduce heat and simmer for 2 minutes over low heat. Mix cornstarch with the cold water; add to scallop mixture, stirring constantly. Add dillweed, cooked rice and mix well. Fill warmed taco shells with the scallop mixture; top with shredded lettuce, grated cheese and chopped tomatoes.

Serves 4

Variation: For **Zesty Scallops***, add several drops of hot pepper sauce to the sauce mixture.

Easterners' Crab Meat Pie

This recipe comes from a very dear friend in Nova Scotia. Great for a potluck.

9"	pastry shell for 1 pie	23 cm

Crab Filling:

6 oz.	crab meat, drained and flaked	170 g
⅔ cup	chopped celery	150 mL
⅓ cup	chopped green pepper	75 mL
1	garlic clove, minced	1
¼ cup	chopped onion	60 mL
2 tbsp.	flour	30 mL
½ tsp.	salt	2 mL
⅓ cup	chili sauce OR pasta sauce	75 mL
2 tsp.	Worcestershire sauce	10 mL

Swiss Cheese Sauce:

2 tbsp.	butter OR margarine	30 mL
2 tbsp.	flour	30 mL
¼ tsp.	EACH salt and paprika	1 mL
¾ cup	milk	175 mL
1 cup	shredded Swiss cheese	250 mL
2 tbsp.	dry white wine	30 mL

Preheat oven to 400°F (200°C). Prepare pastry shell and set aside.

Filling: In a large bowl, combine all of the filling ingredients; mix well and spoon into the pastry shell.

Cheese Sauce: In a small saucepan over low heat, melt butter. Blend in flour, salt and paprika; stir constantly and cook until bubbly, approximately 1 minute. Gradually add milk; cook and stir until mixture boils and thickens. Remove from heat. Stir in ¾ cup (175 mL) of the shredded cheese and the wine. Stir well and pour the sauce over the filling, spreading to cover. Sprinkle with the remaining ¼ cup (60 mL) of cheese. Bake for 10 minutes; reduce heat to 300°F (150°C) and continue to cook for an additional 20-25 minutes, or until bubbly and golden brown. Remove from the oven and let cool for 10 minutes. Cut into wedges and serve.

Serves 4-6

Savory Mediterranean Cheesecake

A sophisticated, tasty dish, leftover chicken and potatoes are combined with sun-dried tomatoes, olives and grated Parmesan.

Potato Parmesan Crust:

2 cups	finely crushed plain potato chips, OR crushed cracker crumbs	500 mL
2 tbsp.	butter OR margarine, melted	30 mL
1 tsp.	dried parsley flakes OR 1 tbsp. (15 mL) chopped fresh parsley	5 mL
¼ cup	grated Parmesan cheese	60 mL

Potato and Chicken Filling:

1 cup	cold mashed potatoes	250 mL
⅓ cup	sour cream	75 mL
8 oz.	cream cheese, softened	250 g
3	eggs, well beaten	3
1 cup	chopped cooked chicken	250 mL
½ cup	pitted black Greek olives, sliced	125 mL
½ cup	stuffed green olives, sliced	125 mL
½ cup	grated Parmesan cheese	125 mL
3	green onions, chopped	3
½ cup	drained, chopped sun-dried tomatoes	125 mL

Crust: Preheat oven to 350°F (180°C). In a small bowl, combine potato chips, melted butter, parsley and cheese; mix well. Press mixture evenly over the bottom of a 9 or 10" (23 or 25 cm) lightly buttered springform pan. Set aside.

Filling: In a large bowl, combine potatoes, sour cream, cream cheese and eggs. Beat with an electric mixer until smooth. Stir in chicken, olives, Parmesan cheese, onions and sun-dried tomatoes; mix well. Spoon the filling evenly over the crust in the pan. Bake for 55-65 minutes, or until cheesecake is browned and firm. Remove from oven and allow to stand for 10 minutes; remove rim. Serve warm or cold.

Serves 8-10

Picnic Portables

Baked Mushroom 'n' Spinach Chicken

Layers of noodles, spinach, mushrooms and chicken in a creamy sauce, this is a great dish for second day chicken.

1 cup	dry bread cubes	250 mL
2 tbsp.	butter OR margarine, melted	30 mL
½ tsp.	garlic powder	2 mL
3 cups	uncooked egg noodles	750 mL
¼ cup	butter OR margarine	60 mL
⅓ cup	chopped onion	75 mL
¼ cup	flour	60 mL
1 cup	milk	250 mL
2¼ cups	chicken broth	550 mL
½ cup	sour cream	125 mL
10 oz.	pkg. frozen chopped spinach, thawed and drained	283 g
10 oz.	can sliced mushrooms, drained	284 mL
2 cups	cooked chicken, cubed	500 mL
1 tbsp.	grated Parmesan cheese	15 mL

Preheat oven to 400°F (200°C). Toss bread cubes with melted butter and garlic powder; set aside. Cook noodles as per package directions; drain and set aside. In a saucepan, melt butter over medium heat; add onion and sauté until soft. Whisk in flour until well blended. Gradually add milk and chicken broth, stirring constantly until thickened. Remove from heat; stir in sour cream. In a 2-quart (2 L) baking dish, layer noodles, spinach, mushroom and chicken. Pour sauce over casserole; top with bread cubes and sprinkle with cheese. Bake for 25-35 minutes, or until sauce begins to bubble. Remove from oven and serve immediately.

Serves 4-6

Pork Fajitas

A tangy Mexican-style pork wrap, cook over a grill, campfire or on a stove.

1 lb.	lean boneless pork	500 g
2	garlic cloves, minced	2
1 tsp.	crumbled dried oregano	5 mL
½ tsp.	cumin	2 mL
¼ tsp.	salt	1 mL
2 tbsp.	EACH orange juice and vinegar	30 mL
6-8 drops	hot pepper sauce	6-8 drops
1 tbsp.	vegetable oil	15 mL
1	EACH onion and green pepper, sliced	1
4	tortillas	4

Slice the pork across the grain into ⅛" (3 mm) strips; set aside. In a large glass bowl or plastic bag, combine garlic, oregano, cumin, salt, orange juice, vinegar and hot pepper sauce; stir and add pork slices. Marinate pork for 10-20 minutes. Heat oil in a heavy frying pan over a grill, campfire or burner; add pork strips and stir-fry until pork is no longer pink, about 3-5 minutes. Add onion and green pepper slices; cook for an additional 2 minutes, stirring frequently. Remove pork from heat and wrap immediately in tortillas. Top with sliced green onions, shredded lettuce, salsa, grated cheese or your favorite toppings.
Serves 4

Sausage 'n' Sauerkraut

A yummy dish for sauerkraut lovers, hearty and comforting.

2 lbs.	ham or garlic sausage, cut into 1" (2.5 cm) slices	1 kg
16 oz	can sauerkraut, drained and rinsed	454 g
16 oz.	can tomatoes with liquid	454 g
1 cup	chopped celery	250 mL
1	large onion, chopped	1
1	large green pepper, chopped	1
3 tbsp.	brown sugar	45 mL
1 tsp.	dried oregano	5 mL
½ tsp	EACH salt and pepper	2 mL

Sausage 'n' Sauerkraut Continued

In a large frying pan over medium heat, sauté sausage cubes until lightly browned, approximately 3-5 minutes. Drain off all fat. Add sauerkraut, tomatoes with liquid, celery, onion, green pepper, brown sugar and seasonings; mix well. Cover and simmer for 20-25 minutes, or until vegetables are tender. Serve immediately over baked or mashed potatoes.

Serves 8-10

Hot and Spicy Pork Bake

This quick and easy savory pork stew may be frozen, but bake before freezing. Thaw overnight in the refrigerator and reheat at 350°F (180°C) for 30 minutes. Wonderful for potlucks or served with pita bread and a green salad.

3 tbsp.	vegetable oil	45 mL
1 lb.	lean pork, cut into strips	500 g
½ lb.	hot Italian sausages, cut into ½" (1.3 cm) slices	250 g
1 cup	sliced onions	250 mL
3	garlic cloves, minced	3
1 cup	frozen peas	250 mL
1 tsp.	salt	5 mL
1 tsp.	ground paprika	5 mL
⅛ tsp.	ground cayenne pepper	0.5 mL
½ cup	long-grain rice	125 mL
1 cup	chicken broth	250 mL
1 cup	tomato juice	250 mL
19 oz.	can chickpeas, undrained	540 mL

Preheat oven to 350°F (180°C). In a large frying pan, over medium-high heat, heat oil and brown pork and sausages; add onions and garlic and cook for 2-3 minutes. Add remaining ingredients and stir to scrape up the brown bits on the bottom of the pan. Pour into a lightly buttered 2-quart (2 L) casserole; bake for 55-65 minutes.

Serves 6-8

Cheese-Stuffed Shells in Herbed Tomato Sauce

Always a hit, this dish is wonderful for potluck, brunch, or patio suppers.

20	jumbo pasta shells, cooked, drained	20
1 lb.	Italian sausage	500 g
1	large onion, chopped	1
10 oz.	pkg. frozen chopped spinach, cooked and well drained	283 g
8 oz.	cream cheese, softened	250 g
1	egg, lightly beaten	1
2 cups	shredded mozzarella cheese, divided	500 mL
2 cups	shredded Cheddar cheese	500 mL
1 cup	cottage cheese	250 mL
¼ cup	grated Parmesan cheese	60 mL
½ tsp.	EACH salt and pepper	2 mL

Herbed Tomato Sauce:

2 x 14 oz.	cans tomato sauce	2 x 398 mL
3 tbsp.	minced onion	45 mL
1½ tsp.	dried basil	7 mL
1½ tsp.	dried parsley flakes	7 mL
1 tsp.	dried oregano	5 mL
3	garlic cloves, minced	3
1 tsp.	sugar	5 mL
½ tsp.	salt	2 mL
¼ tsp.	pepper	1 mL

Preheat oven to 350°F (180°C). Cook and drain pasta shells. In a large frying pan, over medium heat, brown sausage and onion; drain off all fat. Transfer sausage to a large bowl. Stir in spinach, cream cheese and egg. Add half of the mozzarella, all of the Cheddar, cottage, Parmesan cheeses, salt and pepper. Mix well. Stuff shells and arrange in a lightly buttered 9 x 13" (23 x 33 cm) baking dish.

Herbed Tomato Sauce: In a large bowl, combine all sauce ingredients; stir well. Spoon sauce over stuffed shells. Cover and bake for 40 minutes. Remove from the oven; uncover; sprinkle with the remaining mozzarella. Return shells to oven and bake for 5-10 minutes, until cheese melts.

Serves 8-10

Meatballs in Cranberry Chili Sauce

These sweet and tangy meatballs can be made small as appetizers or large for everyday dining. They are great for potluck suppers.

Garlic Soy Meatballs:

2 lbs.	lean ground beef	1 kg
¾ cup	bread crumbs	175 mL
2 tbsp.	dried parsley	30 mL
2	eggs	2
2 tbsp.	soy sauce	30 mL
¼ tsp.	pepper	1 mL
2	garlic cloves, minced	2
⅓ cup	ketchup	75 mL
3 tbsp.	onion, minced	45 mL

Cranberry Chili Sauce:

14 oz.	can whole cranberry sauce	398 mL
1½ cups	chili sauce	375 mL
2 tbsp.	brown sugar	30 mL
1 tbsp.	lemon juice	15 mL

Preheat oven to 350°F (180°C). In a large bowl, combine all meatball ingredients and mix well. Shape into meatballs and place in a 9 x 13" (23 x 33 cm) baking dish. Set aside.

Sauce: In a small saucepan, combine all the sauce ingredients; place saucepan over medium heat and cook, stirring constantly, until the mixture is smooth and the cranberry sauce has melted. Remove from heat and pour sauce over uncooked meatballs. Bake for 35-45 minutes.

Serves 8-10

Note: This dish may also be cooked on the grill. Preheat grill for 10 minutes. Place the meatballs and sauce in a heatproof grilling pan; cover with foil and place over medium heat. Cook as above.

Crusty Mexican Chili Bake

A hot, spicy, tomato bean filling is set on top of a biscuit crust and then topped with cheese, lettuce and tomatoes.

Sour Cream Biscuit Crust:

½ cup	flour	125 mL
½ tsp.	salt	2 mL
½ tsp.	baking powder	2 mL
2 tbsp.	butter OR margarine	30 mL
½ cup	sour cream	125 mL
1	egg, lightly beaten	1

Chili Beef Filling:

1 lb.	lean ground beef	500 g
1	onion, chopped	1
3	garlic cloves, minced	3
1 tsp.	salt	5 mL
2 tsp.	chili powder	10 mL
½ tsp.	hot pepper sauce	2 mL
14 oz.	can kidney beans, undrained	398 mL
½ cup	tomato paste	125 mL
1 cup	tomato sauce	250 mL

Topping:

1 cup	grated Cheddar cheese	250 mL
2 cups	shredded lettuce	500 mL
3	tomatoes, chopped	3
	sour cream and cheese for garnish	

Preheat oven to 350°F (180°C).

Crust: In a large bowl, combine flour, salt and baking powder; stir to combine. With a pastry cutter or 2 knives, cut in the butter until texture is crumbly. Stir in sour cream and beaten egg. Mix well, batter will be slightly lumpy. Turn dough into a lightly greased 9 x 13" (23 x 33 cm) baking pan and spread thinly with the back of a spoon over bottom and sides. Set aside.

Crusty Mexican Chili Bake Continued

Filling: In a large frying pan, over medium-high heat, combine ground beef, onion and garlic. Cook, stirring often, until meat is browned and no pink shows through. Drain off fat; add salt, chili powder, hot pepper sauce, kidney beans, tomato paste and tomato sauce. Stir well and spoon into the crust. Bake for 30-40 minutes; remove pan from oven and sprinkle with cheese. Let stand for 5 minutes; top with lettuce and tomatoes. Serve immediately with sour cream and additional cheese.

Serves 6

Terrific Taco Pie

9"	pastry shell	23 cm
1 lb.	lean ground beef	500 g
½ cup	chopped onion	125 mL
2	garlic cloves, minced	2
10 oz.	can tomato soup	284 mL
1 tsp.	chili powder	5 mL
½ cup	taco sauce OR ketchup	125 mL
1 tbsp.	cornstarch	15 mL
½ cup	shredded Cheddar cheese	125 mL
1½ cups	shredded lettuce	375 mL
1	medium tomato, chopped	1

Preheat oven to 450°F (230°C). Bake pastry shell for 10-15 minutes; reduce temperature to 350°F (180°C) and continue to bake for an additional 10-15 minutes, or until lightly browned. In a large frying pan over medium-high heat, combine beef, onion and garlic. Cook until meat is browned and no pink shows through; drain off all fat. Stir in tomato soup and chili powder. Stir together taco sauce and cornstarch. Stir into meat mixture. Cook and stir until bubbly and slightly thickened. Pour beef mixture into pastry shell and bake for 15 minutes. Remove from oven; sprinkle with cheese and let stand for 5 minutes, or until cheese melts. Top with lettuce and tomato. Serve immediately.

Serves 4-6

Burritos

2 lbs.	lean ground beef	1 kg
1	onion, chopped	1
1½-2 tbsp.	taco seasoning	22-30 mL
¼ tsp.	pepper	1 mL
¼ tsp.	oregano	1 mL
¼ tsp.	parsley	1 mL
1 cup	sour cream	250 mL
4 cups	shredded cheese, Cheddar, Monterey Jack or mozzarella	1 L
¾ cup	taco sauce	175 mL
20	tortilla shells	20

Preheat oven to 350°F (180°C). In a large frying pan, combine ground beef and onions. Place over medium-high heat and cook until meat is browned and no pink shows through; drain off all fat. Add taco seasoning, pepper, oregano, parsley and sour cream. Stir well. Add half of the cheese and half of the taco sauce; mix well. Place 2 heaping tbsp. (40 mL) of beef mixture on each tortilla shell. Roll up and place seam side down on a lightly buttered 9 x 13" (23 x 33 cm) baking dish. Top with remaining cheese and taco sauce. Bake for 20-30 minutes. Serve immediately with sour cream or your favorite toppings.

Serves 8-10

Note: This dish may also be cooked on the grill. Preheat grill for 10 minutes. Place Burritos in a lightly buttered heatproof grilling pan; cover with foil and place over medium indirect heat. Cook as above. Uncover for the last 10 minutes of cooking.

🌲 Keep a pair of heavy gardening gloves in your glove compartment to protect your hands when barbecuing, gathering and chopping wood, etc.

Mexican Beef Bake

Olives add a nice touch to this quick and easy tomato, beef-based casserole. Serve over rice or noodles.

1 lb.	lean ground beef	500 g
¼ cup	chopped onion	60 mL
¼ cup	chopped green pepper	60 mL
2	garlic cloves, minced	2
14 oz.	can tomatoes, chopped	398 mL
1½ cups	whole kernel corn	375 mL
1 cup	tomato sauce	250 mL
1 tsp.	salt	5 mL
2 tsp.	chili powder	10 mL
1 cup	sliced stuffed olives	250 mL
1½ cups	coarsely crushed corn chips	375 mL
½ cup	grated Cheddar cheese	125 mL

Preheat oven to 350°F (180°C). In a large frying pan, over medium heat, combine ground beef, onion, green pepper and garlic. Cook, stirring often, until meat is browned and no pink shows through. Drain off fat; add tomatoes, corn, tomato sauce, salt, chili powder and olives. Mix well and pour into a lightly buttered 2-quart (2 L) casserole. In a small bowl, combine the corn chips and cheese; sprinkle over casserole. Bake for 25-30 minutes.

Serves 6

Note: To bake on a grill, place in a heatproof grilling pan; grill over medium indirect heat for 30-45 minutes.

When camping or backpacking, pack extra large-size garbage bags. In a pinch they can double as rain capes.

Taco-Filled Peppers

½ cup	chopped onion	125 mL
1	garlic clove, minced	1
1 tbsp.	vegetable oil	15 mL
1 lb.	lean ground beef	500 g
1 oz.	pkg. taco seasoning mix	30 g
14 oz.	can red kidney beans, rinsed, drained	398 mL
1 cup	salsa	250 mL
4	green peppers	4
1	tomato, chopped	1
½ cup	shredded Cheddar cheese	125 mL
½ cup	sour cream	125 mL

Preheat oven to 350°F (180°C). In a large skillet, over medium heat, sauté onion and garlic; add ground beef and cook, stirring frequently, until beef is browned and no more pink shows through. Stir in taco seasoning, kidney beans and salsa. Bring to a boil; reduce heat and simmer for 5-10 minutes. Cut peppers in half lengthwise; remove and discard seeds and stems. Immerse peppers in boiling water for 3 minutes; drain. Spoon about ½ cup (125 mL) of the meat mixture into each pepper half. Place peppers in an ungreased 9 x 13" (23 x 33 cm) baking pan. Cover and bake for 15-20 minutes, or until peppers are crisp tender and filling is heated through. Remove the peppers from the oven; top each with chopped tomato, cheese and a dollop of sour cream. Serve immediately.

Serves 4

Note: Peppers may be cooked on the grill. Place in a heatproof grilling pan. Preheat grill for 10 minutes. Place over medium indirect heat and cook for 25-35 minutes. Serve as above.

Grandma Jo's Sloppy Joes

Jo's grandchildren love this dish, so do the big kids!

2 lbs.	lean ground beef	1 kg
1	onion, chopped	1
1	green pepper, chopped	1
2	garlic cloves, minced	2
10 oz.	tomato soup, undiluted	284 mL
15 oz.	tomato sauce	425 mL
¼ cup	brown sugar	60 mL
2 tbsp.	ketchup	30 mL
3 tbsp.	Worcestershire sauce	45 mL
1 tbsp.	prepared mustard	15 mL
1 tbsp.	dry mustard	15 mL
2 tsp.	chili powder	10 mL
10-12	hamburger buns	10-12

In a large saucepan or Dutch oven, over medium heat, brown beef and onions. Cook and stir until no pink shows through. Add green pepper; cook and stir for 5 minutes. Drain off any fat and add all remaining ingredients. Bring to a boil. Reduce heat; cover and simmer for 1 hour, stirring occasionally. Serve on split hamburger buns.

Serves 10-12

For a quick and easy campfire all-in-one meal, in a large square of heavy-duty foil, place chopped potatoes, carrots, onions, niblets corn, peppers, celery, etc., and seasonings of your choice. Add small meatballs or cubed chicken. Gather up the corners of the foil and twist to seal well. Place the foil package on the coals and cook for 30-40 minutes, depending on the size and quantity of vegetable pieces. For faster cooking, keep vegetable pieces small and divide among 3 or 4 packages.

Camp Stew

For those cold rainy days when you need comfort food. Stew and dumplings will do the trick.

2 lbs.	boneless lean beef chuck, round or stew meat, cut into 2" (5 cm) cubes	1 kg
4 cups	water	1 L
1 cup	dry white wine	250 mL
5½ oz.	can tomato paste	156 mL
1 tsp.	salt	5 mL
¼ tsp.	pepper	1 mL
2	onions, quartered	2
1 cup	sliced celery	250 mL
3	carrots, cut into ½" (1.3 cm) rounds	3
4	potatoes, peeled, quartered	4
8 oz.	can whole kernel corn, drained	250 mL

In a large heatproof stew pot, brown meat over direct heat on grill or burner. Add water, wine, tomato paste, salt, pepper, onions and celery; cover and simmer for 1½-2 hours. Add carrots and potatoes; cook 30 minutes longer, or until vegetables are tender. Add corn and heat through. Serve immediately.

Serves 6-8

🌲 Marinate meats by placing meat and marinade in plastic sealable freezer bags and freeze. Pack in a cooler as you set out on your trip. The meat marinates as it thaws.

Sombrero Chili

Hot! Hot! Hot!

¼ cup	flour	60 mL
2 tbsp.	chili powder or more to taste	30 mL
2 tsp.	salt	10 mL
¼ tsp.	pepper	1 mL
2 lbs.	lean boneless chuck or round beef, cut into 1" (2.5 cm) cubes	1 kg
¼ cup	vegetable oil	60 mL
1 cup	chopped onion	250 mL
2 x 19 oz.	cans red kidney beans, drained and reserved	2 x 540 mL
2 x 19 oz.	cans whole tomatoes with juice	2 x 540 mL
2 cups	whole kernel corn	500 mL
¼ cup	sliced pimiento	60 mL
¼ cup	sliced hot chili peppers (optional)	60 mL

In a large plastic or paper bag, combine flour, chili powder, salt and pepper. Shake beef cubes in flour mixture until well coated. In a large saucepan or Dutch oven, add the oil and place over medium-high heat. When oil is hot, brown the floured beef cubes, a few at a time. When meat has all been browned, return it to the saucepan; stir in onion and sauté over medium-low heat for 5 minutes, or until onion is tender. Spoon off any excess oil. Stir in any remaining flour mixture. Add reserved liquid from the kidney beans and add the tomatoes; stir well to break up the tomatoes. Cover and simmer 1½-2 hours, or until beef is tender. Stir in kidney beans, corn, pimientos and chili peppers. Heat just to boiling. Serve over hot rice and sprinkle with Cheddar cheese.

Serves 8

Pictured on page 121.

Dried Chili

Ideal for back packers, make your own camping/hiking provisions.

2 lbs.	lean ground beef	1 kg
1	large onion, chopped	1
2	garlic cloves, minced	2
1	green pepper, seeded, chopped	1
2 x 19 oz.	kidney beans with liquid	2 x 540 mL
2 x 19 oz.	tomatoes, broken with liquid	2 x 540 mL
2 x 5½ oz.	tomato paste	2 x 156 mL
2 tbsp.	chili powder	30 mL
1 tsp.	salt	5 mL
¼ tsp.	pepper	1 mL

Preheat oven to 170°F (77°C). In a large frying pan, over medium-high heat, cook beef, stirring frequently until no pink shows through. Drain off all fat. Add onion, garlic and pepper to the beef. Cook and stir until vegetables are tender-soft. Stir in undrained beans, tomatoes, tomato paste and seasonings. Stir well. Simmer over low heat for 30-45 minutes, stirring occasionally. Taste and adjust seasonings, if desired. Longer cooking may be required to produce a very thick chili. Spread chili thinly on cookie sheets and dry in oven for 8-10 hours. Allow chili to cool and package in resealable plastic bags. Dried chili can be kept for a 2-week period. If longer storage is required, dried chili may be frozen for 3-4 months.

To rehydrate, add 3-4 cups (750 mL-1 L) of water to above dried chili in a large cooking pot. Bring to a slow boil. Add more water if necessary to reach your desired consistency. When the ground beef has softened, about 15-20 minutes, the chili is ready for serving.

Serves 6-8

Note: If chili is packaged in 3-4 smaller packages, add 1-1⅓ cups (250-325 mL) of water per package and reheat as above.

Note: In a convection oven at 140°F (60°C) the drying process takes 6-8 hours.

Grilling or Campfire Cooking

Snacks & Treats

Fish

Chicken

Pork

Beef

Bannock or Biscuits on a Stick

Great for breakfast or with a stew, steak or for a campfire dessert.

2 cups	flour	500 mL
2 tbsp.	baking powder	30 mL
1 tsp.	salt	5 mL
¾ cup	milk OR water	175 mL

In a large bowl, combine flour, baking powder and salt. Add milk and mix until just combined. Flour hands and twist and shape portions of dough around the end of a green stick. Cook over the open campfire until nicely browned. Serve with jam or jelly, or heated pie filling.

Makes 8-10

Variation: Wrap dough around cubes of cooked steak and cook as above. Serve with mustard dip.

Note: You may also try this cooking method with refrigerator biscuits.

Pictured on page 17.

Peanut Butter S'Mores

No campfire is complete without these tasty little morsels.

4	graham crackers	4
2	marshmallows	2
1 tsp.	crunchy peanut butter	5 mL

Roast marshmallows on sticks over campfire or grill until golden brown. Spread 2 crackers with peanut butter; cover each with a roasted marshmallow and top with the remaining cracker.

Serves 2

Campground Potluck Dinner

Sombrero Chili, page 117
Cauliflower and Broccoli Salad with Green Grapes, page 76
Wild Saskatoon Crumble, page 151
Cran Pineapple Punch, page 56

Foil-Roasted Campfire Fruits

Bananas:

2	bananas, peeled	2
2 tbsp.	brown sugar	30 mL
2 tsp.	lemon juice.	10 mL

Peel bananas and place each on a lightly buttered square of heavy-duty foil. Sprinkle each banana with 1 tbsp. (15 mL) of sugar and 1 tsp. (5 mL) of lemon juice. Seal packages and place on medium-hot coals or grill for 10-15 minutes. Remove from foil and serve immediately.

Serves 2

Peaches or Nectarines:

2	peaches OR nectarines, peeled, halved, pitted	2
2 tbsp.	brown sugar	30 mL
2 tsp.	butter OR margarine, melted	10 mL

Peel, halve and pit fresh peaches. Prepare and cook as above, dividing the butter between the peaches, reducing cooking time to 5-7 minutes.

Serves 2

Pictured on the front cover.

Apples:

2	apples, cored	2
2 tbsp.	raisins, washed, dried	30 mL
2 tbsp.	brown sugar	30 mL
¼ tsp.	cinnamon	1 mL
2 tsp.	butter OR margarine	10 mL

Core apples and place each one on a lightly buttered square of heavy-duty foil. Fill each cavity with 1 tbsp. (15 mL) EACH raisins and sugar. Sprinkle ⅛ tsp. (0.5 mL) cinnamon over each apple. Dot with butter. Seal packages and place over medium hot coals or grill for 30-40 minutes, until apples are tender. Remove from foil; serve immediately.

Serves 2

Seafood Kabobs

Use as an appetizer or a full meal deal.

Garlic Butter Baste:

¼ cup	butter OR margarine, softened	60 mL
½ tsp.	paprika	2 mL
3	garlic cloves, minced.	3
4 drops	hot pepper sauce	4 drops
1	large green pepper, cut into 16 pieces	1
1	large onion, quartered, separated into pieces	1
1 lb.	whole fresh mushrooms	500 g
1 lb.	whole cherry tomatoes	500 g
1 lb.	large sea scallops (approximately 16)	500 g
24	jumbo shrimp, shelled and deveined	24

Season a grill with vegetable oil and preheat for 10 minutes to medium.

Baste: In a small grill-safe container, blend all baste ingredients. Mix well and place on the edge of the grill until butter melts. Remove from heat; stir and set aside. Alternate vegetables, scallops and shrimp on 4, 16-18" (41-45 cm) metal skewers. Place kabobs on the grill and brush with the basting mixture. Grill at medium until seafood is opaque and firm, 15-20 minutes; turn kabobs over and brush with baste several times.

Serves 4

Fish in Corn Husks

This cooking method is perfect over a campfire – the fish is moist and flavorful.

cleaned fresh fish, as many as you can catch/eat

Per Fish:

2 tsp.	butter OR margarine	10 mL
2-3 tbsp.	lemon juice	30-45 mL
	salt and pepper to taste	

Fish in Corn Husks Continued

Note: If corn husks are very dry, soak them in water for 5-10 minutes.

In the cavity of each fish, place 2 tsp. (10 mL) of butter. Place each fish in a whole corn husk that has corn and silk removed and husk intact. Sprinkle each fish with 2-3 tbsp. (30-45 mL) of lemon juice, salt and pepper. Wrap husks tightly around fish; tie with a string at the top and place over direct heat on a grill or on a bed of hot coals. Cook for 15-25 minutes, or until fish flakes when tested with a fork. Serve immediately with additional lemon juice or butter.

Variation: Sprinkle fish cavities with salt and pepper. Place a strip of bacon down each side of the fish. Wrap in husks and cook as above.

Pictured on page 85.

Teriyaki Drumsticks

⅔ cup	soy sauce	150 mL
¼ cup	vegetable oil	60 mL
3 tbsp.	brown sugar	45 mL
3 tbsp.	ketchup	45 mL
3 tbsp.	red wine	45 mL
½ tsp.	ground ginger	2 mL
3	garlic cloves, minced	3
12-15	chicken drumsticks, approximately 2½ lbs. (1.25 kg)	12-15

In a large glass dish, combine soy sauce, oil, sugar, ketchup, wine, ginger and garlic; mix well. Add drumsticks and turn to coat thoroughly. Cover and refrigerate for several hours or overnight, turning occasionally. Preheat oven to 375°F (190°C). Drain off marinade and discard. Place the chicken in a single layer in a 10 x 15" (25 x 38 cm) baking pan. Bake for 45-60 minutes, or until chicken is no longer pink.

Serves 6-8

Note: To grill, place chicken in a heatproof grilling pan and cover with foil. Preheat grill for 10 minutes. Place pan over medium direct heat and cook for 55-75 minutes. Remove foil for the last 10-15 minutes.

Sticky Drumsticks

A sweet and sour dish that is fast and easy to prepare, serve this with lots of napkins.

½ cup	apricot jam	125 mL
¼ cup	teriyaki sauce	60 mL
1 tbsp.	brown sugar	15 mL
1 tsp.	cornstarch	5 mL
1 tsp.	cider vinegar	5 mL
¼ tsp.	salt	1 mL
12	chicken drumsticks	12

Preheat oven to 425°F (220°C). In a large bowl, combine all ingredients, except chicken drumsticks, and mix well. Add drumsticks, tossing to coat thoroughly. Spoon chicken and sauce into a well-greased 10 x 15" (25 x 38 cm) baking pan. Bake for 15 minutes; remove from oven and baste chicken with pan juices. Continuing baking, basting every 10 minutes, for an additional 20-30 minutes, or until cooked. Remove the chicken from the oven; baste with sauce again and allow to cool in pan for 10 minutes before serving. To serve, place chicken in a serving dish and spoon the sauce over the chicken.

Note: To grill, preheat grill for 10 minutes. Place chicken and sauce in a heatproof grilling pan; cover with foil and place over medium-hot grill. Cook as above. Uncover for the last 10-15 minutes of cooking.

Serves 6-8

Clean barbecue grills with baking soda. Apply soda with a wire brush and let set for 12-20 minutes. Wipe grills clean. The next fire will burn off any remaining soda or grease.

Chicken and Vegetables in Foil

Moist creamy chicken breasts are cooked with vegetables in foil packets. Delicious!

10 oz.	can cream of mushroom soup	284 mL
½ cup	white wine OR chicken broth	125 mL
½ tsp.	lemon pepper	2 mL
4-6 drops	hot pepper sauce	4-6 drops
4	boneless chicken breasts	4
2 cups	whole green beans	500 mL
2 cups	julienne-cut carrots	500 mL
2 cups	quartered fresh mushrooms	500 mL
2 tbsp.	butter OR margarine	30 mL

In a small bowl, combine soup, wine, lemon pepper and hot pepper sauce; stir well and set aside. Cut 4 sheets of heavy-duty foil, approximately 15-20" (38-50 cm) long. Center 1 chicken breast on each sheet. Spoon mushroom sauce over each. Top with vegetables; dot with butter. Bring up sides of foil and triple fold. Triple fold ends to form a packet, leaving room for heat circulation inside packet. Place foil packets on a grill heated to medium-high; cook for 35-45 minutes. Do not turn packets.

Serves 4

Note: Chicken packets may be baked in a 350°F (180°C) oven, on a cookie sheet, for 25-35 minutes.

Grill whole small zucchini over direct heat or cut large zucchini in half lengthwise. Brush zucchini with olive oil and grill until the skin is charred and the inside is soft.

Baked Parmesan Chicken Breasts

½ cup	butter OR margarine, melted	125 mL
2 tsp.	Dijon mustard	10 mL
1 tsp.	Worcestershire sauce	5 mL
6 drops	hot pepper sauce	6 drops
½ tsp.	salt	2 mL
1 cup	dry bread crumbs	250 mL
½ cup	grated Parmesan cheese	125 mL
6-8	boneless chicken breast halves	6-8

In a shallow bowl or pie plate, combine melted butter, mustard, Worcestershire sauce, hot pepper sauce and salt. Mix well. In a plastic bag, combine crumbs and Parmesan cheese. Dip chicken in butter mixture, then shake in crumb mixture; coat well.

Preheat grill for 10 minutes. Arrange chicken in a heatproof grilling pan, skin side down, in a single layer. Drizzle with any remaining butter mixture. Cover with foil and bake on direct medium heat for 25 minutes; turn chicken and continue baking for an additional 15-20 minutes, uncovered, until chicken is no longer pink and juices run clear. Serve immediately.

Serves 4-6

Note: To bake, preheat oven to 350°F (180°C). Prepare chicken as above; bake, uncovered, for 40-45 minutes.

🌲 Grill halved onions over direct medium heat. Brush with olive oil and grill until tender.

Polynesian Kabobs

Sweet and Tangy! Wonderful as either an appetizer or a main course.

1 lb.	fresh pork sausages	500 g
10 oz.	can whole water chestnuts, drained	284 mL
1	green pepper, cut into 1" (2.5 cm) pieces	1
8 oz.	can pineapple chunks, drained, reserve juice	250 mL
1 lb.	fresh whole mushrooms	500 g

Honey Pineapple Glaze:

3 tbsp.	liquid honey	45 mL
2 tbsp.	reserved pineapple juice	30 mL
2 tsp.	soy sauce	10 mL
1	garlic clove, minced	1
⅛ tsp.	ground nutmeg	0.5 mL

Soak 12, 6-8" (15-20 cm) wooden skewers in water for 30 minutes. Preheat grill for 10 minutes to medium heat. Alternate sausage pieces, chestnuts, green pepper, pineapple chunks and mushrooms on skewers.

To make glaze: In a small bowl, combine all glaze ingredients. Mix well.

Grill kabobs over direct medium heat until sausage is firm and light brown, 10-15 minutes, turning kabobs over and brushing once with glaze .

Serves 4 as a main course or 8-10 as an appetizer

🌲 Grill whole peppers over direct hot heat until the skin is black and bubbled. Cool peppers in a covered container. Peel as soon as cool enough to handle. Slice and sprinkle with olive oil, chopped garlic, basil, oregano, salt and pepper.

Maple-Glazed Ribs

Sweet and tangy! Maple syrup is delicious with pork!

3 lbs.	pork spareribs, cut into 2-rib pieces	1.5 kg
1 cup	maple syrup	250 mL
3 tbsp.	orange juice concentrate	45 mL
3 tbsp.	ketchup	45 mL
2 tbsp.	soy sauce	30 mL
1 tbsp.	Dijon mustard	15 mL
1 tbsp.	Worcestershire sauce	15 mL
1 tsp.	curry powder	5 mL
3	garlic cloves, minced	3
¼ cup	finely chopped onion	60 mL
1 tbsp.	sesame seeds, toasted	15 mL

Preheat oven to 350°F (180°C). Place ribs, meaty side up, on a rack in a 9 x 13" (23 x 33 cm) baking pan. Cover pan tightly with foil. Bake 1¼-1½ hours. Combine remaining ingredients, except sesame seeds, in a saucepan. Place over medium heat and bring to a boil. Reduce heat; simmer for 15 minutes, stirring occasionally. Drain ribs; remove rack and return ribs to pan. Cover with sauce. Bake, uncovered, for 35-45 minutes, basting occasionally. Remove from oven, place on a serving plate and sprinkle with sesame seeds. Serve immediately.

Serves 6

Note: Ribs may be cooked in a heatproof grilling pan covered with foil. Preheat grill for 10 minutes. Cook on direct medium heat as above.

Pictured on page 155.

Honey Garlic Spareribs

Finger licking good!

3-4 lbs.	pork spareribs, cut into 2-rib pieces	1.5-2 kg
1 cup	ketchup	250 mL
½ cup	liquid honey	125 mL
¼ cup	soy sauce	60 mL
4-5	garlic cloves, minced	4-5

Honey Garlic Spareribs Continued

Preheat oven to 300°F (150°C). Place ribs in a single layer in a large baking dish or broiler pan. In a small bowl, combine remaining ingredients and pour over ribs. Cover; bake for 2-2½ hours, basting every half hour. Remove from oven and serve immediately.

Serves 4-6

Note: This dish may also be cooked on the grill. Preheat grill for 10 minutes. Place ribs in a heatproof grilling pan; cover with foil; and place over low indirect heat. Cook as above for 2½-3 hours.

Grilled Ham Steaks with Glazed Apples

Ham steaks topped with apples and a tangy tantalizing glaze.

Caramelized Apple Glaze:

2 tbsp.	butter OR margarine	30 mL
2	apples, cored, sliced	2
½ cup	brown sugar	125 mL
2 tbsp.	corn syrup	30 mL
¼ cup	lemon juice	60 mL
1 tsp.	grated lemon rind	5 mL
½ cup	apple juice	125 mL
3 tbsp.	red wine	45 mL
6	ham steaks	6

In a large frying pan, over medium-high heat, melt butter in pan and add apple slices. Cook quickly until lightly browned. Remove from pan and set aside. Add sugar, syrup and lemon juice to remaining butter in pan; stir until sugar is dissolved. Add lemon rind, apple juice and wine. Boil for 3-4 minutes, or until sauce is thick.

Grill ham steaks over direct heat until heated through, approximately 10 minutes. Transfer to serving plate. Top each steak with apple slices, then the hot glaze. Serve immediately.

Serves 6

Superb Barbecued Steaks

Helpful Hints for the Perfect Steak:

- ✦ Choose one of the choice cuts such as Rib, Rib Eye, Sirloin, Tender-loin, T-Bone, or Strip Loin Steaks.
- ✦ Season steaks but DO NOT add salt before cooking; salt draws out the meat juices.
- ✦ Grease or oil the grill to prevent sticking.
- ✦ To avoid piercing the meat and losing juices, use tongs rather than a fork.
- ✦ Turn steaks ONLY once, or at the very most, twice.
- ✦ For ½-¾" (1.3-2 cm) thickness – COOK PER SIDE – 3-5 minutes for Rare; 5-7 minutes for Medium; 7-9 minutes for Well Done, on medium-high heat.
- ✦ For 1" (2.5 cm) thickness – COOK PER SIDE – 5-7 minutes for Rare, 7-9 minutes for Medium and 9-11 minutes for Well-Done on medium-high heat.
- ✦ Use different plates for raw and cooked meat.
- ✦ Barbecue sauces are best applied toward the end of the cooking time in order to prevent burning.
- ✦ Avoid charring by making sure the grill is as far up from the coals as possible.
- ✦ Preheat barbecue for 10-20 minutes before cooking.
- ✦ For choice-cut steaks, season with pepper or lemon pepper and gar-lic powder OR one of the following Steak Rub recipes. These steaks do not need to be marinated for tenderness. If marinating is desired for flavor, 30-60 minutes marinating time will be sufficient.

Steak Rubs

A rub is a blend of seasonings, such as dried herbs and spices, used to flavor the surface of uncooked steaks and roasts. Sprinkle rub on 10 minutes before cooking, or rub it into the surface of the meat just before cooking.

Steak Rubs Continued

Herb Rub:

1 tsp.	dried basil leaves	5 mL
1 tsp.	lemon pepper	5 mL
½ tsp.	onion powder	2 mL
½ tsp.	garlic powder	2 mL
½ tsp.	dried oregano	2 mL

In a small bowl, combine all ingredients and stir well. Sprinkle or rub over choice-cut steaks or roasts.

Lemon Garlic Rub:

1 tsp.	garlic powder	5 mL
1 tsp.	dried lemon peel	5 mL
1 tsp.	lemon pepper	5 mL
½ tsp.	dried basil	2 mL

In a small bowl, combine all ingredients and stir well. Sprinkle or rub over choice-cut steaks or roasts.

Cajun Rub:

1 tsp.	garlic powder	5 mL
1 tsp.	curry powder	5 mL
1 tsp.	paprika	5 mL
¼ tsp.	cayenne pepper	1 mL

In a small bowl, combine all ingredients and stir well. Sprinkle or rub over choice-cut steaks or roasts.

Mexican Rub:

1 tsp.	chili powder	5 mL
1 tsp.	garlic powder	5 mL
1 tsp.	dried oregano	5 mL
½ tsp.	cumin	2 mL

In a small bowl, combine all ingredients and stir well. Sprinkle or rub over choice-cut steaks or roasts.

Rubbed Steak Parcels

Tender, juicy steaks, this recipe can be cooked on the grill or over the campfire.

6	sirloin steaks	6
2 tbsp.	soy sauce	30 mL
3	garlic cloves, minced	3
1½ oz.	pkg. dry onion soup mix	40 g
1	large onion, sliced	1
1 cup	red wine	250 mL

Rub the steaks with soy sauce and minced garlic. Cover and refrigerate for several hours or overnight. Place each steak on a large sheet of foil. Sprinkle 2 tsp. (10 mL) of soup mix, several onion slices and 2 tbsp. (30 mL) of red wine over each steak. Seal steaks tightly in foil. Grill over direct heat for 8-10 minutes, or until cooked as desired.

Serves 6

Herb-Flavored Butters

Keep a container of premixed herb or flavored butter waiting in your refrigerator, you will find many ways to use it. It is wonderful on grilled meat or fish, vegetables, baked potatoes, sauces and bread, biscuits, or toast.

Herb Butter:

½ cup	butter OR margarine	125 mL
1 tsp.	lemon juice	5 mL
1-3 tbsp.	fresh herbs or half that amount of dried herbs	15-45 mL

Allow butter to soften until you can easily mix in herbs. In a small bowl, combine all ingredients and mix well. Let sit at room temperature for an hour for the flavors to blend. Cover and store in refrigerator. Adding lemon juice accentuates the flavor of many herbs.

Makes ½ cup (125 mL)

Herb-Flavored Butters Continued

Herb Combinations for Butter:
- **chives and garlic**
- **marjoram, thyme and chives**
- **parsley, tarragon and thyme**
- **basil and chives**
- **dill and parsley**
- **tarragon, dill and chives**

Whipped Herb Butter:
Place butter in a small bowl, add any herb combination above. Gradually beat in a small amount of water until mixture is light and fluffy. Cover and store in refrigerator.

Flavored Butters

Sun-Dried Tomato Basil Butter:

½ cup	butter OR margarine, softened	125 mL
¼ cup	oil-packed, sun-dried tomatoes, well drained, chopped	60 mL
⅓ cup	finely chopped fresh basil	75 mL

In a medium bowl, cream butter; add tomatoes and basil. Mix well.

Makes ½ cup (125 mL)

Pictured on the front cover.

Lemon Chive Butter:

½ cup	butter OR margarine, softened	125 mL
4 tsp.	dried chives, crumbled, or ¼ cup (60 mL) chopped, fresh	20 mL
2 tsp.	grated lemon rind	10 mL

In a medium bowl, cream butter; add chives and lemon rind. Mix well.

Makes ½ cup (125 mL)

Helpful Hints for the Less Tender Cuts of Beef

🌲 Less tender cuts of beef include Round, Sirloin Tip, Blade, Cross Rib and Flank steaks.

🌲 For maximum tenderness, marinate steaks in one of the following recipes for 12-24 hours in the refrigerator.

🌲 Pierce steak numerous times with a fork and marinate in approximately 1 cup (250 mL) marinade.

🌲 For maximum tenderness, do not cook steak past medium and, when serving, slice thinly across the grain.

🌲 Use the same cooking guidelines for doneness as for the choice-cut steaks, see page 132.

🌲 Marinating tenderizes and adds flavor to any beef you barbecue. A marinade generally consists of an acidic ingredient such as wine, vinegar, soy sauce, citrus juices, mustard or yogurt plus an oil and a variety of seasonings.

🌲 Marinate beef in a plastic bag or glass dish. DO NOT use metal dishes such as aluminum or iron for marinades. Choose a container in which the beef fits snugly and lies flat.

🌲 Before pouring a marinade on beef, always reserve ¼ cup (60 mL) of the marinade recipe for brushing on the steak while cooking.

🌲 **For beautifully browned steaks, pat with paper toweling before grilling to remove excess moisture.**

Marinade Variations

Far East Steak:

½ cup	barbecue sauce	125 mL
¼ cup	EACH soy sauce and pineapple juice	60 mL
1 tsp.	ground ginger	5 mL
1	onion, chopped	1

Place steak in a shallow dish or plastic bag. In a small bowl, combine all marinade ingredients; stir well. Reserve ¼ cup (60 mL) of marinade. Pour the remainder over the meat; cover and let stand in the refrigerator for 12-24 hours. Remove meat from marinade and cook as per helpful hint instructions.

Greek Steak:

½ cup	barbecue sauce	125 mL
¼ cup	lemon juice	60 mL
1 tsp.	EACH dried oregano and rosemary	5 mL
2	garlic cloves, minced	2

Place the steak in a shallow dish or plastic bag. In a small bowl, combine all marinade ingredients; stir well. Reserve ¼ cup (60 mL) of marinade. Pour the remainder over the meat; cover and let stand in the refrigerator for 12-24 hours. Remove meat from marinade and cook as per helpful hint instructions.

Jacquie's Marinade:

½ cup	soy sauce	125 mL
¼ cup	brown sugar	60 mL
¼ cup	vinegar	60 mL
½ cup	pineapple juice	125 mL
6-8 drops	hot pepper sauce	6-8 drops
3	garlic cloves, minced	3
1	onion, chopped	1

Place the steak in a shallow dish or plastic bag. In a small bowl, combine all marinade ingredients; stir well. Reserve ¼ cup (60 mL) of marinade. Pour the remainder over the meat; cover and let stand in the refrigerator for 12-24 hours. Remove meat from marinade and cook as per helpful hint instructions.

Barbecued Roast Beef

🌲 For choice-cut roasts, Rib, Sirloin, Tenderloin, rub the roast with a garlic clove and sprinkle generously with pepper or lemon pepper.

🌲 For less tender cuts, Round, Sirloin Tip, Rump and Hip roasts, pierce the roast numerous times with a fork, marinate for 12-48 hours in the refrigerator.

🌲 Grill roasts fat side up or cook on a rotisserie over a drip pan in a closed barbecue over indirect medium heat (move coals from directly under the roast, place a drip pan below the meat).

🌲 For Rare, cook 18-20 minutes per pound (40-45 minutes/kg)
For Medium, cook 22-30 minutes per pound (50-70 minutes/kg)
For Well Done, cook 30-35 minutes per pound (75-85 minutes/kg)

🌲 Remove the roast just before desired doneness and allow to sit, covered with foil, for 15 minutes before carving.

🌲 Slice only enough of the roast for the meal. Unsliced leftovers will not dry out as quickly in the refrigerator as sliced.

🌲 Leftover roast beef is tastier if the roast is cooked only to the rare or medium stage.

🌲 Barbecue a roast on the weekend and have fast and delicious leftovers for meals through the week.

Foil-Wrapped Onion and Mushroom Chuck Roast

4 lb.	chuck OR round beef roast	2 kg
¼ tsp.	pepper	1 mL
1½ oz.	envelope dry onion soup mix	40 g
10 oz.	can sliced mushrooms, drained	284 mL
2 tbsp.	red wine (optional)	30 mL

Onion and Mushroom Chuck Roast Continued

Preheat grill to medium hot. Place roast in the center of a large lightly buttered square of double-thick heavy-duty foil. Sprinkle with pepper and soup mix. Cover with mushrooms; sprinkle with wine. Seal well and place on grill or over coals. Bake 2-2½ hours, or until tender.

Serves 8-10

Sukiyaki

An easy "Taste of the Orient" from your grill.

3 tbsp.	vegetable oil	45 mL
¼ cup	chopped green onions	60 mL
1	green pepper, chopped into 1" (2.5 cm) pieces	1
2	garlic cloves, minced	2
1½ lbs.	boneless sirloin steak, cut into thin strips	750 g
16 oz.	can bean sprouts, drained	455 mL
10 oz.	can sliced water chestnuts, drained	284 mL
6	cherry tomatoes, cut in half	6

Soy Ginger Sauce:

¼ cup	water	60 mL
2 tbsp.	soy sauce	30 mL
2 tsp.	cornstarch	10 mL
¼ tsp.	EACH ground ginger, salt and pepper	1 mL

Preheat grill. Place oil in a large cast-iron skillet or grill-safe baking dish and place over heat for 1 minute, or until hot. Add onion, green pepper and garlic. Stir-fry for 2 minutes, or until vegetables are tender crisp. Add beef; cook and stir until beef is no longer pink. Add bean sprouts, water chestnuts and tomatoes. Cook and stir for 2-3 minutes.

Sauce: Blend water, soy sauce, cornstarch, ginger, salt and pepper in a small bowl. Add to beef and vegetable mixture. Cook and stir until thickened and bubbly, 2-3 minutes. Serve immediately.

Serves 4-6

Italian Beef Kabobs

A great all-in-one meal; just add a salad, or use as an appetizer for 8.

Italian Marinade:

1 cup	Italian salad dressing	250 mL
1	small onion, thinly sliced	1
⅛ tsp.	pepper	0.5 mL
1½ lbs.	boneless round steak, cut into 4 x 1" (10 x 2.5 cm) strips	750 g
4	small new potatoes OR 19 oz. can whole white potatoes, drained	4
1	zucchini, cut in ½" (1.3 cm) slices	1

In a small bowl, combine all marinade ingredients. Place beef strips in a shallow glass baking dish or large plastic food storage bag. If using new potatoes, cut in half and parboil for 10 minutes. Drain and add to beef. If using canned potatoes, drain and add to beef. Pour marinade over steak and potatoes. Cover dish or close bag. Refrigerate for at least 4 hours, turning steak and potatoes once.

Preheat grill. Remove meat and potatoes from marinade. Alternate beef, potatoes and zucchini on 4, 14" (35 cm) skewers. Grill over direct heat for 10-15 minutes, turning frequently. Serve immediately.

Serves 4

Don't partially cook meat for later use. To destroy bacteria meat must be completely cooked once you begin the grilling/cooking process.

Hamburger Sauces

Again, three sisters – three sauces, these are all delicious and all very easy.

Jo's Secret Recipe Relish Mayonnaise:

¾ cup	mayonnaise	175 mL
3 tbsp.	dill pickle relish	45 mL
3 tbsp.	ketchup	45 mL

In a small bowl, combine all ingredients and stir well. Refrigerate until serving time.

Makes ¾ cup (175 mL)

Eileen's Zippy Mustard Mayonnaise:

¾ cup	mayonnaise	175 mL
2 tbsp.	prepared mustard	30 mL
1 tbsp.	Worcestershire sauce	15 mL

In a small bowl, combine all ingredients and stir well. Refrigerate until serving time.

Makes ¾ cup (175 mL)

Jacquie's Cucumber Mayonnaise:

½ cup	mayonnaise	125 mL
¼ cup	peeled, seeded, finely chopped cucumber	60 mL
1 tbsp.	finely chopped onion	15 mL

In a small bowl, combine all ingredients and stir well. Refrigerate until serving time.

Makes ¾ cup (175 mL)

Hamburgers

For RVs, camping, at home, hamburgers are easy and quick. With these variations you'll be inspired.

1 lb.	lean ground beef	500 g
1	egg, lightly beaten	1
¼ cup	bread crumbs	60 mL
1	onion, finely chopped	1
¼ tsp.	pepper	1 mL

In a large bowl, combine all ingredients and mix well. Shape into 4-6 evenly shaped flat patties, approximately ¾-1" (2-2.5 cm) thick. Grill until centers are no longer pink, turning once. Cook approximately 5 minutes per side. Well-done burgers are brownish throughout with clear juices. About 1 minute before burgers are done, brush with barbecue sauce, if desired. Serve immediately on toasted hamburger buns and top with desired toppings.

Serves 4

Burger Variations:

Mexican Burger – To the ground beef mixture, add 2 tbsp. (30 mL) dry Taco Seasoning mix; and 1 tsp. (5 mL) garlic powder. Serve burgers with salsa, shredded Cheddar cheese, lettuce and tomatoes. Serve on toasted hamburger buns or soft flour tortilla shells

Greek Burger – To the ground beef mixture, add 1 tsp. (5 mL) EACH garlic powder, dried rosemary and dried oregano. Serve burgers with crumbled feta cheese, chopped black Greek olives, tomatoes, red onions and cucumbers. Serve on toasted hamburger buns or in pita pockets.

Italian Burger – To the ground beef mixture, add 1 tsp. (5 mL) EACH dried oregano and dried basil. Serve burgers with mozzarella cheese, tomato slices, red onion slices, or sprinkle with Italian salad dressing and Parmesan cheese. Serve on toasted hamburger buns or Italian rolls.

Hamburgers Continued

Teriyaki Burger – To the ground beef mixture, add 1 tsp. (5 mL) ground ginger and 1 tbsp. (15 mL) soy sauce. Serve burgers with teriyaki sauce, grilled pineapple slices and bean sprouts. Serve on toasted hamburger buns or sesame buns.

Helpful Burger Tips

- Defrost ground beef in the refrigerator or in the microwave – NEVER on the counter. Cook ground beef as soon as possible after defrosting.
- When camping, remove from the cooler only the amount of raw meat that will fit on your grill at one time.
- Use a gentle touch when shaping ground beef patties. Overhandling will result in a firm compact texture after cooking. For juicy burgers, turn only once and DO NOT press or flatten with spatula while cooking.
- To help patties hold together, place them in the refrigerator for 15-60 minutes before cooking.
- Thoroughly wash the plate that held the raw patties before using it to hold cooked burgers.
- Wash hands and utensils thoroughly before and after handling raw meat.
- When shopping, always pick up meat items last and take directly home and refrigerate. If you do not plan to cook the meat within 2 days, wrap it well and freeze it.

To save time, buy ground beef in bulk and brown it. Divide beef into recipe-sized portions and freeze until needed. It's ready to use for spaghetti sauces, tacos, burritos, etc.

Grilled Beef Pizza

Pizza in a ground beef crust. Delicious for any occasion.

½ lb.	bacon	250 g
2 lbs.	lean ground beef	500 g
1	large onion, chopped	1
½ tsp.	paprika	2 mL
½ tsp.	dried oregano	2 mL
3	garlic cloves, minced	3
¼ cup	tomato paste	60 mL
1½ cups	grated mozzarella cheese	375 mL
½ lb.	fresh mushrooms, sliced	250 g
1	green pepper, seeded, chopped	1
2	large tomatoes, sliced	2
¼ cup	grated Parmesan cheese	60 mL
½ tsp.	dried basil	2 mL

Preheat grill for 10 minutes. In a heatproof pan, grill or fry bacon until crisp; crumble and set aside. In a large bowl, combine ground beef, onion, paprika, oregano and garlic; mix well. Press beef mixture evenly onto a 10-11" (25-28 cm) pizza pan or pie plate. Spread evenly with tomato paste; then layer the cheese, crumbled bacon, sliced mushrooms, sliced pepper and sliced tomato. Sprinkle with Parmesan cheese and basil. Cover with foil, grill for 15 minutes over direct medium heat; uncover and drain off fat. Re-cover and continue grilling until meat is cooked through and cheese is melted, approximately 20-25 minutes. Remove foil for the last 5-10 minutes of cooking. Drain off fat and serve immediately.

Serves 4-6

When grilling vegetables or whole-meals in foil packages, adding 2-3 ice cubes (or more depending on package size) adds moisture and helps prevent burning.

Desserts

Fresh Fruits
Baked Fruits
Cheesecakes
Pies
Cakes

5-Minute Homemade Ice Cream

Wow! Make this fast and easy extra-rich treat in your food processor.

1 cup	whipping cream	250 mL
⅓ cup	sugar	75 mL
1 tsp.	vanilla	5 mL
2 cups	frozen, unsweetened, strawberries, raspberries, or cherries	500 mL

Using a food processor, with the chopping blade, process cream, sugar and vanilla until smooth, about 1 minute. Through the feed tube in the food processor, add frozen fruit, a few pieces at a time; process until smooth. Spoon ice cream into bowls and serve immediately.
Serves 4

Fruit Kabobs with Orange Rum Glaze

A quick dessert or serve these kabobs around the campfire for easy snacking.

1	fresh pineapple, peeled, cored, cut into chunks	1
1 lb.	whole fresh strawberries, cleaned	500 g
3	kiwi fruit, quartered	3
3	bananas, quartered	3

Orange Rum Glaze:

1 tsp.	grated orange rind	5 mL
½ cup	orange juice	125 mL
2 tsp.	lemon juice	10 mL
¼ cup	honey	60 mL
2 tbsp.	rum	30 mL
⅛ tsp.	ground cinnamon	0.5 mL

Skewer all fruit alternately onto 12-14" (30-35 cm) skewers. In a small bowl, combine all glaze ingredients. Brush fruit with glaze and place on grill. Cook for 5-8 minutes, turning frequently and brushing with glaze. Serve hot or cold.

Makes 12 kabobs

Pictured on page 155.

Fresh Fruit Tarts

Use the fruit of the season, or the fruit of the region for these easy dessert tarts.

1 cup	flour	250 mL
½ tsp.	salt	2 mL
⅓ cup	butter OR margarine	75 mL
2-3 tbsp.	cold water	30-45 mL
8 oz.	cream cheese, softened	250 g
3 tbsp.	sugar	45 mL
1 tbsp.	milk	15 mL
¾ tsp.	vanilla	3 mL
	seedless red and green grapes, kiwi fruit, strawberries, raspberries blueberries	
	canned mandarin-orange sections	
	whipped cream, sour cream or yogurt for garnish	

Preheat oven to 425°F (220°C). In a medium bowl, stir together flour and salt. With a pastry blender or 2 knives, cut in butter until mixture resembles coarse crumbs. Sprinkle cold water, 1 tbsp. (15 mL) at a time, into flour mixture, mixing lightly with a fork after each addition until dough is just moist enough to hold together. Shape dough into a ball. Cut dough into 24 pieces. Press each piece evenly into bottom and up sides of 24, 1¾-2" (4.5-5 cm) muffin cups. Prick each pastry cup with a fork. Bake for 15 minutes, or until golden brown. Cool pastry cups for 5 minutes in pans; remove cups from pan and set on wire racks to cool completely.

In a small bowl, combine cream cheese, sugar, milk and vanilla. Beat until smooth. Divide filling among the pastry cups. Fill each cup with your choice of fresh fruit. Garnish each with a dollop of sweetened whipped cream, sour cream or plain yogurt.

Makes 24 tarts

Fresh Peach Pie

This crust and filling is a snap to make in your microwave – the flavor is superb.

Crumb Crust:

5 tbsp.	butter OR margarine	75 mL
1⅓ cups	graham cracker crumbs	325 mL
2 tbsp.	brown sugar	30 mL

Peach Filling:

5 cups	fresh peaches, peeled, sliced, divided	1.25 L
⅔ cup	sugar	150 mL
2 tbsp.	cornstarch	30 mL
¼ cup	water	60 mL
2 tbsp.	lemon juice	30 mL

Crust: Melt butter in a 9" (23 cm) pie plate at 100% (high) for 45-60 seconds. Stir in crumbs and sugar; mix well. Press crumbs firmly and evenly against bottom and sides of plate using a spoon or a smaller pie plate. Microwave at 100% (high) for 1½ minutes; rotate ½ turn after 1 minute. Let cool thoroughly before filling

Filling: Mash 1 cup (250 mL) peach slices with a fork. In a small microwave bowl, combine sugar and cornstarch. Stir in water, lemon juice and the mashed peaches. Microwave at 100% (high) for 2-5 minutes, or until thickened and clear, stirring every minute. Arrange remaining peach slices in cooled crust. Spoon peach glaze over peach slices, spreading carefully to cover. Refrigerate for several hours. Top with whipped cream or ice cream.

Serves 6

Variations: For the crust, substitute finely crushed vanilla wafers, gingersnaps or chocolate wafers for graham cracker crumbs. Decrease butter OR margarine to ¼ cup (60 mL) and omit sugar.

Variation: For **Peach Blueberry Pie**, sprinkle 1 cup (250 mL) of fresh blueberries over the sliced peaches in the crust. Cover with the glaze as above.

Orange and Strawberry Trifle Cake

This recipe comes from Aunt Rene, our favorite aunt. She used to serve this trifle every Christmas Eve in an elegant cut-glass bowl. In this new format it is an easy, attractive dessert that can be dressed up for any occasion.

1	pound cake, cut into ½" (1.3 cm) slices	1
2 x 3 oz.	pkg. orange gelatin powder	2 x 85 g
5 oz.	pkg. vanilla pudding powder	140 g
2 x 10 oz.	frozen sliced strawberries in syrup, thawed, drained	2 x 284 g
1½ cups	whipping cream, whipped OR 1-qt. (1 L) tub whipped topping	375 mL
2 cups	fresh strawberries for garnish	500 mL

Line the bottom of a 9 x 13" (23 x 33 cm) baking dish with pound cake slices. Dissolve gelatin powder according to package directions. Slowly pour over cake, allowing gelatin to soak in, ensuring all cake is covered. Refrigerate until set. Cook pudding according to package directions. Cool completely; pour pudding over cake and gelatin layer, spreading to cover completely. Top with the drained strawberry slices. Cover with whipped cream or whipped topping. Garnish with fresh strawberries.

Serves 12-15

For a Fourth of July Picnic: Arrange blueberries over a square in the top left-hand portion of the cake. Space so whipped cream shows for stars. Arrange sliced strawberries in rows over remaining whipped cream to give red and white stripes.

For a Canada Day Picnic: Cut out a maple leaf pattern. Place pattern in center of cake and trace around it with a toothpick. Place a strawberry tip in each leaf point and arrange remaining fresh, sliced strawberries into a leaf shape.

Polynesian Trifle

Wonderful! Wonderful! Wonderful! Truly a taste of Hawaii.

¼ cup	toasted coconut	60 mL
1	angel food cake	1
6 oz.	pkg. vanilla pudding and pie filling	170 g
19 oz.	can crushed pineapple, drained	540 mL
1 cup	flaked coconut	250 mL
1 cup	chopped Macadamia nuts	250 mL
12 oz.	frozen whipped topping, thawed	340 g

To toast coconut, preheat oven to 350°F (180°C). Spread the coconut evenly on a baking sheet. Place in oven for 3 minutes. Stir and toast for 1-2 minutes longer, or until lightly browned. Remove from oven; spread on a paper towel and allow to cool completely.

Tear cake into bite-sized pieces. Place in an ungreased 9 x 13" (23 x 33 cm) baking pan; set aside. Cook pudding according to package directions. Cool completely. When pudding is cold, stir in drained pineapple and pour over cake pieces in pan. Sprinkle with coconut and Macadamia nuts. Spread with whipped topping to cover completely. Sprinkle with cooled toasted coconut. Refrigerate until ready to serve.

Serves 12-15

🌲 Use powdered milk for baking and cooking. It is light to carry, convenient to store and won't spoil.

Wild Saskatoon Crumble

Saskatoons have a unique tart/sweet flavor but they are not always available. This delicious crumble is very adaptable – try your favorite fruit combinations.

3 cups	saskatoons, washed, drained	750 mL
½ cup	water	125 mL
⅓ cup	sugar	75 mL
1 tsp.	ground cinnamon	5 mL
½ cup	brown sugar	125 mL
½ cup	flour	125 mL
¼ cup	rolled oats	60 mL
¼ cup	butter OR margarine	60 mL

Preheat oven to 375°F (190°C). Lightly butter a 9" (23 cm) square baking pan. Place the saskatoons in the pan; add the water. Combine sugar and cinnamon and sprinkle over the berries. In a small bowl, combine brown sugar, flour and rolled oats; mix well. With a pastry cutter or 2 knives, cut in the butter until crumbly. Spread over the saskatoon mixture. Bake for 55-65 minutes. Serve warm with ice cream.

Serves 6

Variations: Substitute equal amounts of sliced or chopped fruit for the saskatoons. Try apples; peaches and/or blueberries; apples and cranberries; rhubarb and strawberries, etc. Double the first sugar amount if fruit is very tart.

Pictured on page 121.

For a rich-tasting, easy dessert, caramelize bananas by grilling them in their skins. Grill over direct heat until skins are black all over. Slice bananas lengthwise to serve.

Peach Shortcake

*Make this when peaches are in season; it is an absolute must for peach lovers.
The hint of ginger brings out the true flavor of fresh peaches.*

Shortcake:

2 cups	flour	500 mL
2 tbsp.	brown sugar	30 mL
1 tbsp.	baking powder	15 mL
½ tsp.	salt	2 mL
½ tsp.	ground ginger	2 mL
½ cup	butter OR margarine	125 mL
⅔ cup	milk	150 mL

Peach Filling:

1½ lbs.	ripe fresh peaches, peeled, thinly sliced	750 g
6 tbsp.	brown sugar, divided	90 mL
¼ tsp.	ground ginger	1 mL
1 cup	whipping cream, whipped	250 mL
¼ cup	chopped toasted pecans	60 mL

Preheat oven to 425°F (220°C).

Shortcake: In a large bowl, combine flour, brown sugar, baking powder, salt and ground ginger; stir well. With a pastry blender or 2 knives, cut in butter until mixture resembles coarse crumbs. Add milk, stirring only until moistened. Turn dough onto a lightly floured surface; knead 10-12 times. Pat dough evenly into a lightly buttered 8" (20 cm) round baking pan. Bake 20-30 minutes, or until golden brown. Remove the cake from the pan and allow to cool on a wire rack.

Filling: In a large bowl, combine sliced peaches with 4 tbsp. (60 mL) of brown sugar and the ginger; stir well. Whip the cream with the remaining 2 tbsp. (30 mL) of brown sugar until stiff.

Toasted Pecans: Preheat oven to 350°F (180°C). Place pecans in a single layer on an ungreased cookie sheet. Bake 10-15 minutes. Cool in pan.

Pictured on page 35.

Peach Shortcake Continued

To serve: Split shortcake into 2 layers; place bottom layer on a serving platter. Spoon half of the peach mixture over the cake; top with half of the whipped cream. Cover with the second cake layer and remaining peach mixture. Garnish with remaining cream and sprinkle with pecans. Serve immediately.

Serves 8-10

Blueberry Torte

Make this with wild blueberries, if possible. It is twice as good when you have picked the blueberries; you can truly enjoy the "fruits" of your labor.

4	eggs	4
1 cup	sugar	250 mL
½ cup	water	125 mL
1 tsp.	vanilla	5 mL
1 cup	flour	250 mL
2 tsp.	baking powder	10 mL
½ tsp.	salt	2 mL
3 cups	blueberries, fresh or frozen, thawed or wild	750 mL
2 cups	whipping cream, whipped grated orange rind	500 mL

Preheat oven to 375°F (190°C). In a large bowl, with an electric mixer, beat eggs for 2-3 minutes, or until thick. Beat in sugar gradually. Stir in water and vanilla. In a small bowl, combine flour, baking powder and salt. Add to egg mixture, stirring just until combined. DO NOT BEAT. Butter and flour 3, 8" (20 cm) layer-cake tins. Divide batter evenly among cake tins. Sprinkle batter thickly with blueberries. Bake for 15-20 minutes. Remove cakes from pans and cool completely. To serve, spread whipped cream between cake layers. Frost with whipped cream and sprinkle with grated orange rind.

Serves 12-15

Strawberry Delight

Prepare this delicious, easy three-layer dessert at home or in your RV.

Brown Sugar Pecan Crust:

1½ cups	flour	375 mL
1 cup	butter OR margarine	250 mL
¼ cup	brown sugar	60 mL
½ cup	chopped pecans	125 mL

Cream Cheese Filling:

8 oz.	cream cheese, softened	250 g
¾ cup	icing (confectioner's) sugar	175 mL
8 oz.	whipped topping	250 g

Strawberry Topping:

3 oz.	strawberry gelatin powder	85 g
2 x 10 oz.	frozen sliced strawberries, thawed with syrup reserved	2 x 283 g
½ cup	sugar	125 mL
½ tsp.	salt	2 mL
1 cup	strawberry syrup (reserved from frozen strawberries)	250 mL
¼ cup	cornstarch	60 mL

Crust: Preheat oven to 350°F (180°C). In a large bowl, combine all crust ingredients. Mix well. Spread evenly in a 9" (23 cm) square pan. Bake for 15- 20 minutes. Remove crust from oven; set aside to cool.

Filling: In a large bowl, beat cream cheese and icing sugar together. Fold in whipped topping and spread over cooled crust.

Topping: Make strawberry gelatin as directed on package; refrigerate until partially set, then spread over the filling. Drain strawberries and measure 1 cup (250 mL) of syrup. In a saucepan, over medium-low heat, combine sugar, salt, strawberry syrup, sliced strawberries and cornstarch. Cook, stirring constantly, until the mixture comes to a boil and thickens. Allow to cool. Spread the strawberry glaze over the gelatin layer. Refrigerate for 6-8 hours before serving.

Serves 8-10

Saturday Night Dinner in the RV

Maple-Glazed Ribs, page 130
Grilled Cheesy Vegetable Zucchini Boats, page 92
Fruit Kabobs with Orange Rum Sauce, page 146

Layered Lemon Supreme

A luscious lemon filling tops an almond shortbread crust.

Almond Crust:

1 cup	flour	250 mL
½ cup	butter OR margarine	125 mL
⅓ cup	ground almonds	75 mL
2 tbsp.	sugar	30 mL

Creamy Lemon Filling:

8 oz.	cream cheese, softened	250 g
½ cup	icing (confectioner's) sugar	125 mL
1 tsp.	vanilla	5 mL
1 cup	whipped cream, whipped OR 8 oz. (250 g) of whipped topping	250 mL
7½ oz.	pouch lemon pie filling mix	713 g
¼ cup	sliced almonds	60 mL

Crust: Preheat oven to 350°F (180°C). In a large bowl, with a pastry cutter or 2 knives, combine flour, butter, ground almonds and sugar. Mix until dough forms a ball. Press into the bottom of a 9 x 13" (23 x 33 cm) baking pan. Bake for 15-20 minutes, or until golden brown. Remove from the oven and set aside to cool.

Cheese Layer: In a large bowl, beat cream cheese, icing sugar and vanilla together until smooth. Fold in half of the whipped cream or whipped topping. Spread over the cooled crust.

Lemon Filling: Prepare the pie filling according to package directions. Cool to lukewarm, stirring occasionally. Spread over the cheese layer. Refrigerate until cool. Spread remaining whipped cream or whipped topping over the lemon layer. Refrigerate. Garnish with sliced almonds just before serving.

Serves 12-15

Chocolate Caramel Cheesecake

This cheesecake is loaded with toasted pecans, creamy caramel, chocolate filling and topped with whipped cream, a perfect ending for your barbecue.

Caramel Crumb Crust:

2 cups	vanilla wafer crumbs	500 mL
½ cup	butter OR margarine, melted	125 mL
14 oz.	pkg. caramels, unwrapped	400 g
¾ cup	half-and-half cereal cream OR evaporated milk	175 mL
2 cups	chopped pecans, toasted, divided	500 mL

Chocolate Filling:

4 x 8 oz.	cream cheese, softened	4 x 250 g
1 cup	sugar	250 mL
2 tsp.	vanilla	10 mL
4	eggs	4
1 cup	semisweet chocolate chips, melted, slightly cooled	250 mL
1 cup	whipping cream, whipped	250 mL

Preheat oven to 350°F (180°C).

Crust: In a small bowl, combine vanilla wafer crumbs and melted butter; blend well. Press into the bottom and 2" (5 cm) up the sides of a 10" (25 cm) springform pan. Bake for 8-10 minutes, or until set. Remove from the oven and set aside to cool. In a saucepan, over low heat, melt caramels in cream, stirring until smooth. Cool for 5 minutes. Pour over crust and top with 1½ cups (375 mL) of chopped pecans.

Filling: In a large bowl, beat cream cheese until smooth. Add sugar and vanilla; mix well. Add eggs, 1 at a time, beating well after each addition. Add chocolate; mix just until blended. Carefully spread the chocolate filling over the pecans. Bake for 55-65 minutes, or until filling is almost set. Remove the cheesecake from the oven and cool to room temperature. Chill overnight in refrigerator. Garnish with whipped cream and remaining ½ cup (125 mL) of toasted pecans.

Serves 16-18

Special Occasion Menu Suggestions

Canada Day Barbecue

Seafood Kabobs, page 124
Prime Rib Beef Steaks, page 132
Apple and Bacon Baked Beans, page 98
Baked Potatoes
Grilled Cheesy Vegetable Zucchini Boats, page 92
Mediterranean Red Onion Salad, page 78
Orange and Strawberry Trifle, page 149
Double Chocolate Cookies, page 24
Cran Pineapple Punch, page 56
Chilled Apple Tea, page 57

Potluck Block Party

Roasted Garlic Chickpea Dip (Hummus), page 66
Mexican Party Spread, page 69
Easterners' Crab Meat Pie, page 101
Cheese-Stuffed Shells in Herbed Tomato Sauce, page 108
Hot and Spicy Pork Bake, page 107
Picnic Coleslaw, page 81
Layered Lemon Supreme, page 157
Strawberry Delight, page 154
Lemon Lime Concentrate, page 56
Cran Orange Slush, page 61

Special Occasion Menu Suggestions

Picnic In The Park

Tzatziki with Pita, page 67
Party Muffuletta, page 43
Stuffed Cherry Tomatoes, page 63
Mexican Deviled Eggs, page 63
White Chocolate Chunk Cookies, page 25
Peach Champagne Cocktail, page 59

Mandy's Birthday Party

Honey Cinnamon Popcorn Mix, page 6
Grandma Jo's Sloppy Joes, page 115
Corn Dogs with Honey Mustard Sauce, page 48
Super Moist Chocolate Cake, page 32
5-Minute Homemade Ice Cream, page 146
Purple Cows and Pink Cows, page 57

Father's Day Fishing Trip

Cajun Nut and Cereal Snack Mix, page 6
Beef 'n' Garlic Cabbage Buns, page 50
Fish In Corn Husks, page 124
Grilled Corn In Husks, page 91
Campfire Potatoes, page 96
Peanut Butter Crunchies, page 29
Cran Pineapple Punch, page 56

Friday Night Weekend Getaway in the RV

Make Ahead

Blueberry and Banana Muffins, *page 14*
Oatmeal Butterscotch Crisps, *page 18*
Mediterranean Red Onion Salad, *page 78*
Baked Potato Salad, *page 87*
Lemon-Lime Concentrate, *page 56*

Friday Night Dinner at Campsite

Grilled Rib Steaks, *page 132*
Baked Potato Salad, *page 87*
Parmesan Green Bean Stir-Fry, *page 95*
Mediterranean Red Onion Salad, *page 78*
Oatmeal Butterscotch Crisps, *page 18*
Coffee

Saturday Morning Breakfast

Orange Slices
Scrambled Cheddar Dogs, *page 40*
Blueberry and Banana Muffins, *page 14*
Coffee

Friday Night Weekend Getaway in the RV

Saturday Lunch

Hot Dogs with Mustard and Onions
Oatmeal Butterscotch Crisps, page 18
Sliced Apples
Lemon Lime Concentrate, page 56

Saturday Dinner

Chicken and Vegetables in Foil, page 127
Parmesan Potatoes in Foil, page 95
Sprouts with Vegetable Julienne, page 75
Fresh Peach Pie, page 148
White Wine
Coffee

Weekend Shopping List

alfalfa sprouts	lemon juice
aluminum foil	lemon pepper
apples	milk
brown sugar	mushroom soup, canned
butter or margarine	mushrooms
carrots	mustard, prepared
celery	onions
celery salt	oranges
Cheddar cheese	Parmesan cheese
chicken breasts	peaches
coffee	pepper
cornstarch	peppers, red and green
eggs	potatoes
French Dressing, bottled	salt
garlic	steaks, rib
graham cracker crumbs	sugar
green beans, whole	white wine
hot dog buns	wieners
hot pepper sauce	

Shopping List — Stocking RV for Summer Holiday

aluminum foil

baking powder

baking soda

basil, dried

beans, canned

beef broth, packaged

butter or margarine

candles

carrots

cheeses, assorted

chicken broth, packaged

chickpeas, canned

chili powder

cinnamon, ground

coffee

coffee whitener

corn, canned

cornstarch

crackers, assorted snacking

dill pickles

dillweed, dried

eggs

flashlight

flashlight batteries

flour

fruit juices

garbage bags

garlic powder

garlic salt

gelatin powders

ginger, ground

graham crackers

handy wipes

honey

hot pepper sauce

jam

ketchup

lemon juice

lemon pepper

mandarin oranges, canned

marshmallows

matches

mayonnaise

milk, canned/powdered

Shopping List — Stocking RV for Summer Holiday

mushroom soup, canned

mustard, prepared

napkins

nutmeg, ground

oil, vegetable

olives

onion flakes

onions

oregano, dried

paper towels

toilet paper

pepper

plastic containers

plastic storage bags

plastic wrap

potatoes

powdered milk

puddings, packaged

rice

salad dressings, packaged

salmon, canned

salt

soda drinks

soups, dry, packaged

soy sauce

sugar

tea

tomato paste, canned

tomato sauce, canned

tomato soup, canned

tuna, canned

vanilla

vinegar

Worcestershire sauce

Camping Tips

🌲 Always carry 2 pots, 1 for cooking and 1 for boiling water.

🌲 Transfer or re-package all of your supplies into light plastic bags or containers. Leave all excess packaging at home.

🌲 Mix what you can at home and pack in plastic bags or containers.

🌲 Add Dumplings to stews and soups. Combine 1 cup (250 mL) of biscuit mix with ⅓ cup (75 mL) of powdered milk mix and pack in a plastic bag. If desired, add ½ tsp. (2 mL) of your favorite dried herbs. At campsite, add ⅓ cup (75 mL) of cold water and mix. Drop by tablespoonfuls (15 mL) of dough into your simmering stew or soup; cover and cook, without peeking, for 10 to 15 minutes.

🌲 Make up your own soup bases at home. Combine 1 tbsp. (15 mL) of your favorite bouillon mix with ¼ cup (60 mL) dehydrated vegetables, 2 tbsp. (30 mL) quick-cooking angel hair pasta, broken into small pieces, and ⅛-¼ tsp. (0.5-1 mL) of your favorite herbs or spices. Mix and place in a plastic bag. At campsite, add soup mix to 1 cup (250 mL) of boiling water; stir. Cover and allow to stand 5-7 minutes.

🌲 Always carry extra packs of dried soup for emergencies.

🌲 Combine instant pudding powders with powdered milk mix and pack in a plastic bag. At campsite, add cold water and shake until pudding is mixed. Allow to set for 5-10 minutes.

🌲 Always pack a small variety of your favorite herbs and spices. They can liven up most dishes.

🌲 There are a variety of quick cooking pasta and sauce mixes on the market that only require adding milk or water. They are great for "One-Pot-Meals"; just add canned meats, fish, seafood, vegetables, cheese or herbs.

🌲 Instant oatmeal packs well and may be combined with any number of fresh or dried fruits or berries, nuts, raisins or spices to provide a substantial breakfast.

🌲 Dried fruits, granola bars or trail mix are great for snacking and will provide a quick source of energy.

🌲 Pack coffee singles or you can get powdered instant coffee in any number of flavors, cappuccino or expresso.

Index

Index 169

Share A Taste of the Great Outdoors

Order at $14.95 per book plus $3.00 (total order) for postage and handling.

A Taste of Brunch – number of books_____ x $14.95 = $ ____
A Taste of Christmas – number of books _____ x $14.95 = $ ____
A Taste of the Great Outdoors – number of books ____ x $14.95 = $ ____
Shipping and handling charge _____ = $ 3.50
Subtotal _____ = $ ____
In Canada add 7% GST OR 15% HST where applicable _____ = $ ____
Total enclosed_____ = $ ____

U.S. and international orders payable in U.S. funds / Price is subject to change.

NAME:_____
STREET: _____
CITY: _____ PROV./STATE _____
COUNTRY _____ POSTAL CODE/ZIP_____

Please make cheque or money order payable to:
Three Sisters Publishing Inc.   **www.3sistersbooks.com**
12234 – 49 Street
Edmonton, Alberta, Canada   T5W 3A8

For fund raising or volume purchase prices, contact
Three Sisters Publishing. Please allow 3-4 weeks for delivery.

Share A Taste of the Great Outdoors

Order at $14.95 per book plus $3.00 (total order) for postage and handling.

A Taste of Brunch – number of books_____ x $14.95 = $ ____
A Taste of Christmas – number of books _____ x $14.95 = $ ____
A Taste of the Great Outdoors – number of books ____ x $14.95 = $ ____
Shipping and handling charge _____ = $ 3.50
Subtotal _____ = $ ____
In Canada add 7% GST OR 15% HST where applicable _____ = $ ____
Total enclosed_____ = $ ____

U.S. and international orders payable in U.S. funds / Price is subject to change.

NAME: _____
STREET: _____
CITY: _____ PROV./STATE _____
COUNTRY _____ POSTAL CODE/ZIP_____

Please make cheque or money order payable to:
Three Sisters Publishing Inc.   **www.3sistersbooks.com**
12234 – 49 Street
Edmonton, Alberta, Canada   T5W 3A8

For fund raising or volume purchase prices, contact
Three Sisters Publishing. Please allow 3-4 weeks for delivery.

Other books available from Three Sisters Publishing Inc.

For best results, share the good food in all of these books with good friends.

A Taste of Christmas – A Treasury of Holiday Recipes, Menus, Customs, Crafts and Gift-Giving Ideas

by Jacquie Schmit, Eileen Mandryk, Jo Wuth

Enhance the special magic of Christmas with the tantalizing aromas of Christmas baking and heartwarming gifts of homemade delicacies. Tempting recipes use make-ahead suggestions for easy preparation. Menu ideas for the whole holiday season include festive brunches, buffets and dinners. Included are numerous ethnic recipes and Christmas customs from many parts of the world.

Retail $14.95 6" x 9"
172 pages 8 colour photographs
ISBN 1-895292-85-9 perfect bound

A Taste of Brunch – Beautiful, Versatile, Year-Round Brunches

by Jacquie Schmit, Eileen Mandryk, Jo Wuth

Beautiful brunches – treat yourself and your family, enjoy your own parties with this superb collection of easy-make recipes. Casual or elegant; cottage, garden, deck or townhouse, these brunch menus and recipes offer great flexibility year-round. On a relaxed weekend morning you can indulge in your favorite breakfast, snack and lunch dishes. This second book from *The Taste of Christmas* authors offers a new selection of no-fuss, satisfying dishes with many make-ahead options.

Retail $14.95 6" x 9"
172 pages 8 colour photographs
ISBN 1-894022-33-5 perfect bound